Introduction to the
Summa Theologiae
of Thomas Aquinas

Other Titles of Interest from
St. Augustine's Press and Dumb Ox Books

Introduction to the
Summa Theologiae
of Thomas Aquinas

The Isagogue of John of St. Thomas

John of St. Thomas [John Poinsot]

Translation and Introduction by
Ralph McInerny

ST. AUGUSTINE'S PRESS
South Bend, Indiana
2004

Manufactured in the United States of America.

1 2 3 4 5 6   10 09 08 07 06 05 04

Library of Congress Cataloging in Publication Data
John of St. Thomas, 1589–1644.
Introduction to the Summa theologiae of Thomas Aquinas / the Isagoge of John of St. Thomas; translated with a preface by Ralph McInerny.
p.   cm.
Includes bibliographical references.
ISBN 1-890318-70-1 (alk. paper)
1. Theology, Doctrinal – Early works to 1800. 2. Thomas, Aquinas, Saint, 1225?–1274. Summa theologica. 3. Catholic Church – Doctrines – Early works to 1800. I. Title.
BX1749.J64 2001
230'.2 – dc21   2001002549

∞ The paper used in this publication meets the minimum requirements of the American National Standard for Information Sciences – Permanence of Paper for Printed Materials, ANSI Z39.48-1984.

Table of Contents

Preface

John of St. Thomas (1589–1644) was the last major figure in the revival of scholasticism that took place in the sixteenth and seventeenth centuries, largely in Spain. He was born John Poinsot in Lisbon on July 9, 1589, his father an Austrian, his mother of Portuguese nobility. He attended the University of Coimbre, receiving his Master of Arts at the age of eighteen and then, because his father's service with the Archduke Albert of Austria took him to Flanders, John's education was continued at the University of Louvain. In 1608, he began studying theology under a Spanish Dominican, Thomas de Torres. Under this tutelage, a Dominican vocation was born, and John entered the Order of Preachers in Madrid, in 1612. The following year, he began his long career at the University of Alcala, teaching philosophy and theology in the Colegio de Santo Tomas. His philosophical works were gathered into the *Cursus Philosophicus Thomisticus* in three volumes, Madrid, 1637, a work that has been reprinted into our times. (The edition by B. Reiser appeared from 1930 to 1938.)

After teaching philosophy for seventeen years, John was appointed to the Chair of Prime, which he occupied for eleven years when he was appointed to the even more prestigious Vespers Chair of theology. His theological work occupies eight volumes, only three of which appeared during the lifetime of John, the rest being gathered after his death. Called the *Cursus Theologicus*, it began to appear in 1637, has been reprinted many times, most recently the incomplete edition prepared by the Benedictines of Solesmes, from volume one of which the work here translated is taken.

After but two years in the Vespers Chair, John was chosen by King Philip IV of Spain as his confessor, and he reluctantly left the university. At court, he continued leading the austere life of a Dominican friar and studying theology. On a military campaign in Catalonia, John came down with fever and died at Fraga, June 15, 1644, just short of his fifty-fifth birthday.

The pedigree of Thomism runs from Sylvester of Ferrara (1474–1528), whose commentary on the *Summa contra Gentiles* is included in the critical Leonine edition of that work, through Thomas de Vio, Cardinal Cajetan (1469–1534), and then into the Iberian school, Francisco de Vitoria (1492–1546), Domingo de Soto (1495–1560), Melchior Cano (1509–1560), Luis de Molina (1535–1600), Domingo Banez (1528–1604), Gabriel Vasquez (1549–1604), and Francisco Suarez (1548–1617).[1] Molina, Suarez, and Vasquez were Jesuits, the others were Dominicans, but they worked in a common intellectual ambience created by Vitoria's restoration of philosophy and theology at Salamanca. The dispute *de auxiliis*, on human freedom and divine causality, which pitted Dominican against Jesuit, has captured the notice of contemporary scholars. But it was the influence of St. Thomas Aquinas on all these men that characterized the revival. The *Summa theologiae* replaced the *Sentences* of Peter Lombard as the work on which the aspiring theologian must cut his professional teeth. Accordingly, we find a great number of close commentaries on parts and treatises of the *Summa*. All Vitoria's published works were posthumous, and each is occupied with a single topic; his reflections on the moral implications of Spanish colonization in America have earned him enduring fame. Domingo de Soto's writings reflect the fundamental importance Aristotle, his logical and other writings, held in the revival. In theology, de Soto commented on the *Sentences*, but in his independent treatise on justice, he bases himself closely on the Treatise on Law of the *Summa*, but not so closely as to exclude the introduction of quite new themes that seem to have been dictated by the concept of rights employed by Vitoria. Cano is most known for his *De locis theologicis*, an enumeration and discussion in descending order of importance of the authoritative reference points for theology. Molina commented on parts of the *Summa*, but is most known for his

1   These are the major figures. They were surrounded by a host of others. Clemente Fernandez, s.j., in his *Los filosofos escolasticos de los siglos XVI y XVII*, Madrid: Biblioteca de Autores Cristianos, 1986, includes texts of all the major figures. On the others, see Guillermo Fraile, o.p., *Historia de filosofia española*, Vol. 1, *Desde la época romana hasta fines del siglo XVII*, Madrid, BAC, 1985.

writings on free will and grace. Banez, like de Soto, commented on works of Aristotle as well as on parts of the *Summa*. With Vasquez we get *Commentaries and Disputations on the First Part* of St. Thomas's *Summa*. One can perhaps discern here a progressive movement away from close exegetical readings of the text of Thomas toward a looser and more commodious disputation in which contemporary issues could be more easily included. With Suarez, it might be said, there is complete autonomy vis-à-vis any one authoritative text, both in philosophy and theology.

The *Disputationes Metaphysicae* (1597) are today the most familiar work of Suarez. In many ways, Suarez is the culmination of the movement to which we have been referring. Historians have pointed out the influence of Suarez, and of Francisco Toledo, on the education received by René Descartes. Suarez did not write as a disciple of anyone but sought to find the most adequate answers by appeal to a vast range of sources. A criticism of him, one that John of St. Thomas would make, is that Suarez is an eclectic. What John of St. Thomas sought to do was to return philosophy and theology to a primary allegiance to the thought of Thomas Aquinas, but Suarez's style had a decisive influence on John.

One might expect a Thomist of the strict observance to engage in the kind of close commentary on the text that characterized Thomas's own commentaries on Aristotle, or Cajetan's on the *Summa*, but in both his philosophical and his theological work, John writes in relative independence of the text that prompts the discussion. He will summarize rapidly the relevant work of Aristotle, and then go on to a discussion guided as much by later controversy as by the text itself. So, too, there is in the theological writings a kind of *tour de monde* survey of what others have said on the question before launching into his own solution. But the vast theological effort was prefaced by three sizeable essays: an analysis of the *Sentences* of Peter Lombard, a discussion of the authority the thought of St. Thomas enjoys in the Church, and the analysis of the *Summa theologiae* translated here. The full title is: *Isagoge ad D. Thomae theologiae. Explicatio connexionis et ordinis totius Summae Theologiae D. Thomae, per omnes ejus materias.*

John's introduction is just that – it is not a commentary or

analysis of the text of the *Summa theologiae,* but a bearing of its
infrastructure, displaying the ordering principles that
brought together the vast treasury of Christian theology in as
economical and perspicuous a manner as possible. In many
ways, John's task was simple: all he had to do was pick up on
the quite overt remarks of St. Thomas as to why a topic or
treatise comes before or after others, what the inner ordering
of a treatise was, what the ordering of the articles within a
question was, and, not to put too fine a point on it, why the
objections in a given article come in the order they do. The
Summa theologiae was written for theological, though not
philosophical, beginners, and it aims to give a swift, accurate,
and adequate sense of the theological terrain. From that point
of view, John can be said to have provided an outline of an
outline. This is not to disparage what he has done. There are
enormous advantages to being acquainted with the skeleton
of the *Summa* before examining the flesh that covers it. There
is no need to overstate John's achievement to see it as something for which the neophyte can be grateful and which, even
for one who thinks himself an adept, not only reinforces the
old sense of the storied order of the *Summa* but, in its hurried
and pedestrian prose, contains more than one precious
nugget absent from more ambitious commentaries.

The translation is made from the Solesmes edition: *Joannis
a Sancto Thoma,* O.P., *Cursus theologicus,* Tomus primus. Opera
et studio Monachorum Quorundam Solesmensium O.S.B. edi-
tus, Paris, 1931, pp. 142–219. As far as I know, the only other
translation is by M. B. Lavaud, O.P., *Introduction à la théologie
de S. Thomas* (Paris: Blot, 1928). Half a century ago, I found
Lavaud's translation in a bookstore in Quebec and, as I read
it, thought it would be useful to have an English translation
as well. The thought persisted down the years, and here at
last is the result.

Ralph McInerny
University of Notre Dame

Prologue

"In order that our task might be contained within certain limits, it is necessary first to ask of sacred doctrine what it is and what its scope is."

No attentive reader of this *Summa of Theology* can doubt that Saint Thomas excels all the other doctors of the Church of God in putting order into the teaching of sacred wisdom, and for this reason can lay claim to wisdom since, according to Aristotle, the proper task of the wise man is to order.[1] The ordering of sciences is like the dispositions an architect makes in laying the foundations of a building. Thus, the Apostle says of himself (1 Corinthians 3, 10–11): "As a wise builder I laid the foundation. And indeed: For other foundation no one can lay, but that which has been laid, which is Christ," as the Apostle adds in the same place. On this foundation the whole theological edifice is elevated; for divine wisdom looks to no other object and foundation than divine clarity's immense light, whose illuminating splendor shines forth, lifts up, and enlightens our mind and intellect: "Its light was like to a precious stone, as it were a jasper-stone, clear as crystal." (Apocalypse 21, 11) That is why this light must be artfully ordered and disposed by a wise architect if faith is to be built up: if this light, which comes forth and descends from heaven, is said to be like a stone, this is not because it emits rays like the sun, but insofar as polished and adapted to a fitting edifice, its light and truth become manifest. Thus the prophet Isaiah divinely foretells the Church when he says (chap. 54, 11–13): "behold I will lay thy gates of graven stones, and all thy borders of desirable stones. All thy children shall be taught of the Lord: and great shall be the peace of thy children." By this symbol and allegory of stones, the prophet expresses the words of divine wisdom. Jerome clearly

---

1   Aristotle, *Metaphysics* I, 2, 982a17.

explains the text "I will base you on sapphires," which in the Septuagint reads, "I will prepare a ruby for you" (*On Isaiah*, Book 15)[2] : "The ruby that is prepared or laid out in an orderly way, he says, seems to me to be the fired word of doctrine, dispelling the shadows of error and thus enlightening the hearts of believers." The words of the prophet seem to signify this vividly enough, when he explains those precious stones: "All your children shall be taught of the Lord." Therefore by speaking of stones he speaks metaphorically of the ordered disposition of things, the effect and end of which is the doctrinal formation of all the children of the Church.

Therefore this great ministry of laying out the stones of celestial wisdom in orderly fashion, although many of the holy Fathers and doctors of the Church labored at it, was arranged by divine providence that it be brought to happy consummation chiefly by Saint Thomas Aquinas. For in this *Summa of Theology*, with heavenly help, he ordered the whole of theology, wonderfully disposing those precious stones in such a way that nothing more wisely or congruously ordered can be imagined: "Look and make it according to the pattern, that was shewn thee in the mount," as Moses said. (Exodus, 25, 40) Or as David, who traced out the measure of the temple to be built according to a celestial plan: "All these things, said he, came to me written by the hand of the Lord, that I might understand all the works of the pattern." (1 Chronicles 28, 19) That is why the chief and most efficacious way of entering into and grasping the mind of the Angelic Doctor in this wonderful edifice of theology is by first diligently seeking the order he followed in the disposition and treatment of his *Summa*, proceeding from one question to the next, from one matter to another, as if joined by golden links. No one rightly merits the name of wise master who ignores the order of the science he would teach. But as Ambrose beautifully admonishes (in commenting on the verse "Instruct me in the way of your decrees" of Psalm 118, 27): "To act knowingly and not know the order of making, is not perfect knowledge,

---

2   *On Isaiah.* Migne, *Patrologia Latina*, 24, col. 524.

for disorder offends. Thus ignorance of the plan upsets the nature of inquiry and detracts from merit. But he who first learns the mysteries of God and then the order of the mysteries, penetrates the wonderful things of God."[3]

Therefore, with confidence in divine help, we will try to lay out in a general way the marvelous order of the whole *Summa of Theology* and the interconnection of treatises and topics that Saint Thomas himself discovered and perfected, as well as the questions making up the treatises, briefly showing the object of each and the place they occupy in the whole work.

3   *Patrologia Latina*, 15, col. 1245.

BOOK ONE

THE THREE PARTS OF THE *SUMMA*
AND THEIR TREATISES

Overview of the Summa

FIRST PART
GOD

1. The Divine Essence. Qq. 1–26
2. The Trinity of Persons in God. Qq. 27–43
3. The Procession of Creatures from God. Qq. 44–119

FIRST PART OF THE SECOND PART
MORALS IN GENERAL

1. Ultimate End. Qq. 1–5
2. Means to the End. Qq. 6–114
    A. Human Acts. Qq. 6–48
    B. Intrinsic Principles. Qq. 49–89
    C. Extrinsic Principles. Qq. 90–114

SECOND PART OF THE SECOND PART
MORALS SPECIFICALLY

1. What Is Common to All. Qq. 1–171
    A. Theological Virtues. Qq. 1–46
    B. Cardinal Virtues. Qq. 47–170
        Prudence. Qq. 47–56
        Justice. Qq. 57–122
        Fortitude. Qq. 123–140
        Temperance. Qq. 141–170
2. Particular States of Life. Qq. 171–189

THIRD PART
CHRIST THE SAVIOR

1. Incarnation. Qq. 1–26
2. Life, Passion, and Death. Qq. 27–59
3. Sacraments. Qq. 60–90

Chapter 1

Why Are There Three Parts of the *Summa*?

Saint Thomas's Introduction (*ST*, I, 1, 1)

In order to establish a scientific procedure for theology, Saint Thomas was always careful to proceed from the more to the less common, from causes to the caused, and from the more known to the less known. Therefore, in the very first and introductory question, he considers the science itself, explaining its necessity, dignity, specification, and mode of proceeding. Second, he considers the object of this science, discussing the various matters with which the science is concerned and the order among them, an order needed just because they are various and diverse. As for the formal object, no ordering is needed, since it is one. The formal object of any science is that which orders, not that which is ordered. But it was necessary for him first to treat the science itself and then its object, since beginners in any science must first be taught the usefulness and worth of that science before disputes about particular matters can be treated.

Division of the Material Object of Theology

Having discussed in the prefatory question the science itself of theology, Thomas sets out to plumb the depths of the object to be explained. This is to set out upon the deep, as Ambrose explains[1] when discussing Christ's words to Peter,

---

1 Commentary on Luke, Book IV, chap. 5. *Patrologia Latina, 15, col. 1693.*

"Put out into the deep, and lower your nets for a catch."
(Luke 5, 4) The object of theology is profoundly deep, for it is
God himself, God as God, in all the fullness of his being, that
is, not just this or that attribute, for example, wisdom or justice, but the very essence and formality of deity along with all
his attributes, for God is "an infinite ocean of being," as Saint
Gregory of Nazianzus put it.[2]

Given an object so deep and profound, Thomas first
divides it into two aspects: its being and its causality, and fittingly enough, since activity follows on being. As Saint
Thomas remarks elsewhere:[3] "Although knowledge of the
created effects of God comes before knowledge of God for the
natural theologian, for the theologian, consideration of the
Creator takes precedence over the consideration of creatures." Although the principal theological concern is God's
being, the theologian spends more time discussing God as
causing and the things caused by him, since in this life we
know God through the mirror of creatures and the darkness
of his effects.

The treatment of God as causing, as the cause of creatures,
fittingly excludes two of the four kinds of cause, namely,
material and formal (in the sense of informing and constituting a nature). The material cause is excluded because it is
based on potentiality, which is repugnant to the pure act God
is; the formal or informing cause is excluded because it
implies dependence and inferiority, either to the whole it constitutes (the whole is greater than its part) or to the subject in
which it inheres. Since God is the most perfect being, and
pure act, he is inferior to nothing, nor does he depend on anything. As for the other two causes, namely, the efficient and
final, Saint Thomas considers three modes of causing which
provide a division of the whole theological order.

First, God is an efficient cause, insofar as he produces,
conserves, and governs things.

Second, God as final cause, not just the universal end of

2   Second Prayer for Easter. *Patrologia Latina,* 36, col. 626.
3   Prologue to the Exposition of Boethius's *On the Trinity.*

all creatures – something Saint Thomas treats briefly when he considers the way things proceed from God (See First Part, q. 44) – but much more importantly as he is the particular end of the rational creature, by whom he is attainable and for whom he is an object of joy through acts of intellect and will. Thus it is that creatures not only proceed from God but return to him from whom they have come. But the rational creature fell from his proper dignity by sin and became like irrational creatures in not returning to God, stuck in the enjoyment of created goods and turned away from God. "Man living in wealth and not understanding, is like unto the beasts that perish." (Psalm 48, 21)

That is why in a third way God causes and acts as repairing the effects of sin which turned man from his ultimate end, something only God can do. Just as to be separated from the first efficient cause is annihilation, which only God can prevent, who sustains all things "by the word of his power," so to turn from the ultimate end, which is to sin, is something only God, who cleanses us from our sins, can repair. These two are opportunely conjoined by the Apostle when he says of the Son of God, "by whom also he made the world; who being the brightness of his glory and the image of his substance, and upholding all things by the word of his power, has effected man's purgation from sin . . ." (Hebrews 1, 3) His efficient causality is signified by "upholding all things" and his role as redeemer by "has effected man's purgation from sin."

So it is that Saint Thomas, by this threefold consideration of God as cause, namely as effective principle (Part One), as finalizing happiness (Part Two), and as redeeming Savior (Part Three), divides the whole *Summa theologiae*. (This is clear from the second question of the First Part.) Thus from God considered in himself and in his being, we pass to God as efficient and redemptive cause, in order to come back to him as the object of happiness after the glorious resurrection. So it is that the golden circle of theology is closed.

Chapter 2

The Connection of the Treatises in Each of the Parts

The First Part
God in Himself and God as Efficient Cause.

There are then three principal parts of the *Summa theologiae*, in the first of which Saint Thomas, after considering God in himself, goes on to consider him as the efficient cause of creatures.

1. The study of God in himself is divided into two treatises, the first of which, On the One God (*De deo uno*), has for its object God in his essence and in his absolute attributes, whether entitative or operative (**qq. 2–26**), the second of which, On the Triune God (*De deo trino*), has for its object the divine relations, the mystery of the Holy Trinity (**qq. 27–43**).

2. The study of God as efficient cause has three subdivisions.

a. In the first, the productive activity itself is considered, God's creative causality, as well as some general things about God as exemplar and final cause of all creatures (**qq. 44–46**).

b. The second considers the effects that come from God, whose variety constitutes the universe. This diversity, which is, as it were, infinite, is here considered under two heads: First, with respect to good and evil, that is, the perfected and unperfected or defective. Second, with respect to the spiritual and corporeal, and mixed cases of these. Angels are purely spiritual, the bodies of this world made in the course of the Six Days are corporeal, whereas man is a mixture of the corporeal and spiritual. All these, their natures and essences, as well as their properties and activities, and their being brought into existence, are treated in **qq. 47–102**.

c. The third is concerned with the governance whereby God conserves creatures and acts on them, whether by immediately moving them or by acting on them through intermediaries. The creatures through which God governs this universe are, first, the angels, through whom he enlightens and teaches others and rules corporeal things. Second are the heavenly bodies, by whose movement lesser bodies are generated and corrupted. Third, there are men, who can act on others, both because of their soul and because of their body. Of this governance of God, immediate or mediated, he treats in **qq. 103–119**, which bring the first part of the *Summa* to a close.

The Second Part
God as Final Cause.
Human Activity, or Man's Return to His End.

Man, writes Saint John Damascene, is said to be made in the image and likeness of God, insofar as by image is meant an intellectual being having free will and power over himself. Having considered the exemplar, namely God, and the things which proceed from the divine power according to his will, we must consider his image, that is, man, insofar as he is cause of his own works, as having free will and power over them. (Prologue to *ST* IaIIae)

The second part is very extensive and is subdivided into two huge sub-parts, one of which is called the First Part of the Second Part (*Prima Secundae*) and the other the Second Part of the Second Part (*Secunda Secundae*). In this second part Saint Thomas considers God as he is attainable by the rational creature through his own acts, acts by which he either tends to his end, if his acts are good, or deviates and turns away from it, if they are sins: this is the basis of the subdivision of the second part.

First, Saint Thomas treats the ultimate end itself, and this is God, in **qq. 1–5**. Second, the acts themselves, whereby we tend to or recede from the end, but this is in turn subdivided, since he first considers these acts in general, with respect to what contributes to and is needed for their morality – this takes up the whole First Part of the Second Part. Then he treats acts in particular, with respect to the different virtues or vices from which they proceed. This is the concern of the Second Part of the Second Part.

The Treatises that make up the First Part of the Second Part
God as Last End. Human Activity in General.

Moral acts in general are considered in the First Part of the Second Part, and this in two respects. First, with respect to the acts themselves and their morality. Second, with respect to the principles by which they are formed, directed, or from which they proceed.

1. Human Acts
Morality is the regulation of free acts by precepts and rules of reason. Hence the formal note of morality in such acts is that they are regulated, the material note that they are free and voluntary. Only free acts are susceptible to regulation by reason; for what comes about necessarily has no need to be regulated by intellect. Morality is found in some acts properly and as such, and in others secondarily and by way of participation.

It is found properly and as such in acts proceeding from the rational powers, namely, intellect and will, where the notion of the voluntary is first and as such found (by way of origin in intellect, formally in will). By way of participation and secondarily acts of sensitive appetite, that is, the passions, can be voluntary. As for acts which are voluntary as such, they are various but form an order among themselves.

For some are absolute, such as the simple act of will (*voluntas*); others discursive, such as *intention*, which does not look to the end absolutely but as attainable by certain means; and *choice*, which looks to the means as ordered to the end. There are other acts which are required for choice and follow on it, such as *consent, counsel, use, command*, and so on. In such acts a man acts rationally, that is, moved from one thing to another discursively, some being prior and efficacious such that others follow from them. For that reason, the first are called *interior acts*, and those that follow on them are called *exterior acts*, being, as it were, outside these and moved and commanded by them. This is the basis for Thomas's procedure in treating moral acts from **qq. 6–21.**

Here then is the order Saint Thomas follows in his treatment of moral acts: He begins with the voluntary and involuntary, which are required for morality from the point of view of matter. Then he treats of absolute acts of will and the causes that move the will. Next, he treats formal elements and modalities insofar as they affect the commanding or interior acts and commanded or exterior acts. Finally, he treats the properties consequent on morality, such as merit and demerit, praise and blame, and the like. But because morality is also found in a secondary and participated way in acts of sensitive appetite, insofar as they are moved by reason (these acts are generally called passions, because they come about with some corporeal change, such as love and hate, sadness and joy, hope and fear, and so on), he treats of passions and their properties in **qq. 22–48.**

2. The Principles of Human Acts

After these considerations of human acts in themselves (whether essentially voluntary acts or those such by participation, namely, the passions), Saint Thomas studies the principles of human acts considered in a general way and under two headings. Some interior principles elicit acts which move exterior acts. These eliciting principles are either powers of the souls or habits (*habitus*) superadded to them. Powers are natural properties of the soul itself, and these were treated in the First Part, where human nature, on which they follow, was studied. There remains only to consider the eliciting principles which are habits. They are first treated generally, and then according to their division into virtues and vices and their properties. Finally he treats vices and sins, which are opposed to the virtues (**qq. 49–89**).

The principles which move the human agent from outside are called external or extrinsic, not because they are incapable of effecting something within the soul, but because if they do so this is an effect of God acting on the soul from without. They are of two kinds. Some move by instructing with respect to the object, as is the case with law – for it pertains to law to give knowledge of what is to be done or avoided. Others move by coming to the aid of our weakness, communicating the power to act, which is what grace does. Thus there are two treatises: On law (**qq. 90–108**) and On grace and its effects (**qq. 109–114**).[1]

The Treatises that make up the Second Part of the Second Part
Human Activity in Particular.

Here Saint Thomas considers the human acts whereby we tend toward or deviate from the end, treating them particularly in their various virtues and vices. That he might treat in an orderly way the immense variety of kinds of human act,

---

1   Lavaud points out that these divisions of the IaIIae are stated clearly in the text. The divisions can be stated schematically as follows:
1. The final end and happiness (qq. 1–5: Treatise on Happiness)
2. Human acts in general:
    i. In themselves
        * acts proper to man (qq. 6–21; the second treatise)
        * acts common to men and animals (qq. 22–48; the third treatise)
    ii. In their principles
        * interior acts: virtuous or vicious habits (fourth treatise)
        (this actually comprises three treatises:)
        Habits in general;
        Habits in particular (virtues and gifts);
        Habits in particular (sins and vices).
        * exterior: God moving us to the good, by instruction, the law (fifth treatise), by helping us (sixth treatise)

Saint Thomas deals first with those human acts which pertain generally to every man whatever his condition: these are the virtues and vices of which all men are capable; he then goes on to those which pertain to particular states of life, in which different ministries or offices or professions are exercised. On this basis, the Second Part of the Second Part is subdivided into two.

1. Virtues and Vices

He distinguishes seven principal virtues and as many vices, and he links to the virtues the Gifts of the Holy Spirit which correspond to them. Other less-important virtues depend on these seven, and there are particular vices opposed to them.

There are three theological virtues, faith, hope and charity. These, along with the corresponding gifts and their opposed vices are studied in **qq. 1–46.**

The other four are the cardinal virtues, prudence, justice, fortitude, and temperance. They are called cardinal because they are more important and prior, not absolutely, but in the hierarchy of the moral virtues. Each of them, in a determined domain, observes a chief mode, or must conquer a great obstacle. Many other virtues come under them as potential parts, imitating in less difficult and important matters the act proper to the cardinal virtue to which they are attached. The cardinal virtues, their potential parts, and the Gifts of the Holy Spirit corresponding to them, as well as the vices opposed to them, are studied in **qq. 47–170.**

2. The States of Man

Saint Thomas treats the states or spiritual ministries theologically, not politically; that is, not those which pertain to the civil republic, but only those found in the ecclesiastical polity or regime. He treats of states or ministries insofar as they pertain to the body of the Church and are distinguished by the Apostle (1 Corinthians 12, 4–6) into three kinds: "There are different graces and different ministries and different operations."

Different graces. – The reference is to graces gratuitously given or charisms which are not common to all, such as prophecy, tongues, the gift of preaching, healing, and so on. (These are studied in **qq. 171–178**.)

Different operations. – These follow on the different kinds of life, active and contemplative – the active work of Martha is one thing, the contemplative work of Mary another – and their respective perfections. The two lives and everything related to them are studied in **qq. 179–182**.

Different ministries. – These are the ecclesiastical offices or states. "God has made some apostles, some doctors, others pastors . . ." (Ephesians 4, 11)

Thomas does not treat here of offices or ecclesiastical honors because these belong to other treatises. Ecclesiastical honors or offices imply either powers of order or powers of jurisdiction; the powers of order are studied in the treatise devoted to the sacrament of Holy Orders; the different powers of jurisdiction determined by canon law fall to the domain of the jurists, that is, to those who treat the offices of legate, archdeacon, dean, and others. Saint Thomas is concerned with them here only to the degree that they have for their end the realization of the spiritual perfection of the Church. The study of the less-perfect matrimonial estate belongs to the treatise on the sacrament of marriage. A twofold state of perfection is distinguished: that of bishops who by their office ought to devote their whole life to the perfection of others and who for that reason are supposed to be themselves perfect; that of religious, who by the profession of vows, seek to achieve personal perfection. These are treated in **qq. 183–189**, and conclude the Second Part.

The Third Part

God as Savior.

In the third part Saint Thomas considers God both as repairing the defects of sin by which we fail to seek him and as the way by which we achieve the ultimate end of our salvation. This is to consider God not as creating but as saving, that is, the Incarnate Word. Thomas divides this part into four principal treatises.

The first is *On the Incarnation*, in which the following are considered: The incarnation itself, with respect to the Person assuming human nature, and to the nature assumed; the perfections assumed with this nature (such as grace, knowledge, power, merit, and so forth), and the imperfections or infirmities which for the time the Word left in the nature assumed, in order that the work of redemption might be accomplished; and finally the duties we owe him, such as adoration. All this from **qq. 1–26**.

The second concerns the way in which the Incarnate Word lived among us: his entry into this world by being born from the womb of the Virgin Mary; the course of his life on earth, his relations with the men he instructed by word and example; the benefits he brought; his exit from this world through his passion and death which won our salvation; his return to the Father by whom he was crowned with glory and honor, sitting at his right hand on high. All this is treated in **qq. 27–59**.

The third treatise concerns the means or instruments by which Christ the Lord applies this salvation and justification to us. These are the sacraments, by which we profess our faith in him and which unite us efficaciously with God. These symbols or practical signs, which from our side are professions of faith, are, from the side of God who uses them as instruments, efficient principles of grace by virtue of the blood of Christ. Saint Thomas first considers the sacraments in general, beginning with Question 60, and then he devotes a special study to each of them, **qq. 60–90**. He had completed the part on penance when a cruel and premature death dried up the celestial flow of his words and interrupted the plan of his great theological work. What is lacking in the treatment of the sacraments is supplied by borrowing from his *Exposition of the Sentences* (**Supplementum, qq. 1–68**).

The fourth treatise concerns the end to which we come through the Incarnate Word, namely, an eternal and perfect happiness in the resurrection of the body and the glory of the soul (**Supplementum, qq. 69–99**).

These are the principal parts of the whole of theology and

its general divisions. Now we must show the order and connection of all these topics, taking them up one by one.

BOOK TWO

DETAILED ANALYSIS OF THE
THREE PARTS OF THE *SUMMA*

Detailed Outline of the First Part

The First Part

The Order and Connections of Its Treatises

God in Himself and as Efficient Cause

The Divine Nature

Having in the first question treated in a prefatory manner of the science of theology, as we pointed out above, Saint Thomas begins in the second question to treat of the object of this science, which is God as he is in himself. Here the question whether he is (*an est*) precedes the question as to what he is (*quid est*). Whether he is Thomas treats in a single question, (Ia, q. 2), first by showing that "God exists" is demonstrable and then setting forth demonstrations (the Five Ways) which show this.

Having treated whether God is, the investigation into the quiddity of God begins. Saint Thomas begins by treating first what belongs to God absolutely (up to **q. 27**), then of things that belong to him relatively (*On the Trinity*).

1. On the One God*

In this first treatise, where God is considered in the unity of his nature, one should notice the profundity with which Saint Thomas orders and classifies the divine attributes. He distinguishes three classes of them:

---

*   Editor's Note: The outline form superimposed on the text follows Saint Thomas's *Summa*, not John. It is meant as an aid to the reader.

* Entitative attributes
* Attributes of passive knowability: everything is knowable insofar as it is and by reason of its very entity.
* Operative attributes, concerning:
  ** immanent action (*ad intra*),
  ** transitive action (*ad extra*)
  (Operation is especially proper to the nature just insofar as it is a nature.)

Inquiring into the basis for these distinctions, we should notice the root of them all, namely the very notion of pure act, by which God is absolutely the first being. Potential being is posterior to completely actual being, because potency is perfected by act. Hence the absolutely first being or God cannot be potential because by "God" we understand the first and absolutely most perfect being. If God were in any way potential he would not be absolutely pure act, because the part of him which was potentiality would not be God. Nor would he be absolutely the first being, but some secondary being, namely, potential being. If God were not pure act he would not be wholly the first and most perfect being.

There are two ways of considering pure act. First, in transcendental mode, insofar as uncreated or divine being, who is pure act, is commonly related to essence and attributes. (That which is common to the nature and the properties is transcendental in respect to them, much as created being is transcendentally related to those things which belong to the creature.) Second, in the manner of a nature, insofar as it is understood as something in God constituting his grade and nature, distinct from the properties and attributes. The constitutive difference of any nature is to be sought in its proper activity, because nature is the principle of motion or operation. But understanding is the proper and per se activity of God, because he is maximally immaterial and removed from potentiality. Hence Saint Thomas treats of God or pure act under the concept of nature when he explains that his proper activity is understanding (**q. 14**), which is not distinct from the nature because of its high perfection and the purity of its act.

a. Entitative Attributes

That is why he first explains pure act under the transcendental aspect of uncreated being or of divine substance insofar as this character is common to all the attributes which belong to him as uncreated being and distinct from created being. And we say they pertain to the entitative existence of God, which is uncreated existence.

1. Five Primordial Entitative Attributes

From the notion of pure act conceived as uncreated being arise five principal and, as it were, radical attributes pertaining to the very existence of God. They remove from the notion of pure act five conditions or defects of created and potential being, namely, composition, imperfection, limitation, change, and division or plurality. By means of the attributes which remove these conditions, we know God by way of negation (*remotio*). The five attributes are: Simplicity, which is opposed to composition; Perfection which is opposed to imperfection; Infinity, opposed to limitation; Immutability, opposed to change; Unity, opposed to division or plurality.

By the very fact that he is pure act without any potentiality, nothing can minimize, make imperfect, limit, or determine that act or perfection. Hence greater or lesser is not found in him, and consequently neither whole and parts, because every whole is greater than its part: so he lacks composition.

He lacks imperfection because if any perfection were lacking to him he would be in potency to it, and thus would not be pure act.

He lacks any limitation because if he is in potency to nothing, he is not limited, for limitation arises from some potentiality which does not permit complete actuation and perfection.

He lacks mutability because he is subject to no change, there being no potentiality in him.

Finally he lacks multiplication or division because if he were divided, some perfection would be in one part that was not in the other, and vice versa. Therefore God is one, because he is pure act.

2. Secondary Entitative Attributes

From the above attributes, which are more rooted in entity, three others follow as accessories or consequences of them.

Goodness follows on perfection because anything is good or appetitible insofar as it is perfect. From his perfection in himself it follows that he is communicative of himself, the perfection of others as their end.

Immensity follows on infinity, as infinity of quantity and the reason for his presence in every place, although infinity of being does not suffice for this presence in all things; there must also be infinity of operation and action, which involves only a virtual contact, since he cannot touch something save by giving or effecting, and because he is divine. Since he is immense, he should bestow all things, even existence, which is what anything possesses most intimately.

Eternity, finally, follows on immutability, since what is immutable does not have a duration that can be measured by motion and time, but only by eternity. Although truth is one of the transcendentals it pertains to passive knowability and therefore is treated by Saint Thomas after the treatise on the being of God **(q. 12)**; formal truth pertains to the act of intellect and therefore is treated after the treatise on intellection **(q. 16)**.

This then is the order in which Thomas teats the entitative attributes: First, the simplicity of God which is opposed to created composition **(q. 3)**. Next, perfection **(q. 4)**. Because goodness follows on perfection, he treats it in a twofold way: first, in general **(q. 5)**, then in particular the divine goodness **(q. 6)**. Third, he treats of entitative infinity **(q. 7)**. And because infinite quantity or immensity follows on infinity, he treats of that next **(q. 8)**. Fourth, immutability **(q. 9)**. Because eternity follows on immutability, he treats that next **(q. 10)**. Finally, he treats of the unity of God **(q. 11)**.

b. Attributes of Passive Knowability

Saint Thomas next treats the attributes of passive knowability, which is as his transcendental truth. First he treats God's passive knowability rather than of God as knowing. The reason is that passive knowability is something more universal, since it is found in every being, and follows on the transcendental concept of his being, by reason of which he is called knowable, whereas to be knowing pertains to operating and follows on a determinate level of nature, for nature is the principle of operating. Fittingly, then, Saint Thomas treats God's passive knowability prior to his active knowing. But since passive knowability relates to some knower, God's passive knowability can be compared either as ordered to the divine intellect as knowing (and since this supposes God as knowing and understanding actively, it is considered under the heading of God's knowledge) or it can be compared to the created intellect as knowing God, which comes about maximally in the beatific vision, and this he treats in **q. 12**. But because knowledge of God is presupposed to naming him – we name a thing insofar as we know it – he discusses the names of God and the way in which names signify him in **q. 13**.

c. Operative Attributes
He next discusses those attributes which belong to the operative order, that is, God's knowledge considered under the aspect of nature, or the constitutive grades of nature. The notion of nature is formed from operation, the principle of which in created things is nature. In God of course there is no principle of the kind involved in the relation of first act to second, but only the pure and ultimate actuality of operation itself. If different attributes of intellection are distinguished – such as wisdom, prudence, and the like – these are based on particular relations to objects or on the manner of attaining them, not on the very act of intellectuality, which pertains to the grade of nature.

Since there are two kinds of operation, immanent and transient, Saint Thomas first considers immanent operation (**qq. 14–24**) and only afterward takes up transitive or executive operation (**q. 25**). Immanent action is naturally prior to transitive, both because it is more intimate to the agent and because the immanent is directive whereas the transitive is executive, and execution presupposes direction.

1. Immanent Divine Operations

Here is the way in which Saint Thomas distributes attributes which involve the immanent operation of God. First, he treats those which belong precisely and uniquely to intelligence, since understanding precedes willing. Second, he treats those which belong precisely to will and its operations and virtues. Third, he discusses mixed attributes, involving both intellect and will, which belong to one power as moved by another, such as providence or prudence pertain to intellect as commanding and ordering, which presupposes and is moved by the efficacy of will, without which providence would be rendered ineffective and in vain. There is no need to treat of other immanent actions because only operations of intellect and will are found in God; immanent operations which pertain to bodily senses are not found in him.

a. Attributes Pertaining to Intelligence Alone (qq. 14–18)

The order of discussion is as follows. First Saint Thomas considers understanding as such and its specification, the objects to which it extends (q. 14). Then, he considers perfections which belong to understanding by reason of intellectuality, both on the side of the subject and on the side of the object. On the part of the subject, perfection of life belongs to the one understanding, because understanding is a vital operation, that is, belongs to the living. On the part of the object, the chief perfection of the one understanding is truth, since to lack the truth or to be in error is a great imperfection. Truth is known and pursued only by intellect, either as already formed and proceeding from it in the way that things made proceed from art and take their truth from conformity with the rules of art. For this an exemplar or idea is required, since art effects the thing thought of. Therefore, after considering the divine understanding, Saint Thomas turns to life, truth, and ideas as perfections of the divine intellectuality.

He treats the ideas first, then truth, and last, life, their interconnections requiring this order of teaching. Because in the question concerning God's knowledge Saint Thomas showed that God's knowledge is the cause of things, and that it is practical knowledge with reference to creatures, he must immediately display those principles which are exemplars or ideas with respect to the intellect which is formative of creatures. Next he treats truth, which is found in creatures transcendentally in conformity with the divine ideas or exemplars, by which natural things are formed, as it were, in the way in which artifacts are made by the artisan. Formal truth, on the other hand, pertains to judgment and is found only in intellect. Finally, he treats of life which pertains to the subject that understands: by understanding, he lives. He considers ideas in **q. 15**, truth in **q. 16** and its opposite, falsity, in **q. 17**. He considers God's life, which is the perfection of the subject that knows, in **q. 18**.

b. Attributes Pertaining to Will Alone (**qq. 19–21**)

Saint Thomas begins his treatment of attributes which pertain absolutely and precisely to will in **q. 19**. He divides the study as follows: First, he treats of will itself, recognizing in God a true and proper elicited appetite which takes its rise from knowledge. He turns next to the acts of will and then to the virtues attributed to it. Saint Thomas first considers the will itself and then its acts – those he did not take up in discussing intellect (q. 14). The act of intellect does not have the note of operation save as the highest and ultimate actuality of intellectuality, and since nature in God is constituted by the highest level of understanding, being pure act, Saint Thomas does not treat the act of understanding separately from the nature of intellect itself. The act of willing does not constitute nature but presupposes intellectuality as already constituted. That is why volition – since it does not constitute nature – carries the note of operation rather than rank of being, whereas intellection pertains to the rank of being of pure act rather than to operation. That is why it is explained without reference to the eliciting principle which is will; this also shows that will in

God is an elicited not a natural appetite. So he considers first will in itself (**q. 19**) and then its acts and virtues.

Acts of will are distinguished in two ways. First, with respect to the desirable object, as fit to be loved, or unfit and to be avoided, in the way in which love and hate, hope and joy, and the like are distinguished. Second, the distinction of acts is based not on the desirable as such, but on the desirable as ruled and measured by reason. This is the way the different moral virtues are distinguished, because the object of morality is the desirable – what can be willed – as regulated.

Thus Saint Thomas distinguishes two kinds of act or virtue in the divine will, and first precisely as ordered to the desirable under the note of fitting or unfitting, in order that it be loved. These he treats in **q. 20**, considering love and joy in God; as for the others, which pertain to flight from or difficulty in the object, they are not formally and directly found in God because they are imperfect.

In the following question (**q. 21**) he considers the virtues of the divine will according to the notion of morality: in God these come down to two, justice and mercy. For the moral virtues concern either the passions as ordered by reason or activities that relate us to others. The first sort, temperance, fortitude, and so on, cannot belong to God except metaphorically since they are in the passions. Hence mercy itself, insofar as it implies the passion of sadness occasioned by the misery of another, belongs to God only metaphorically. Those belonging to acts that refer to others, such as justice, liberality, and so forth, can be found in God so long as they do not imply subjection to a superior, such as religion, observance, and the like, but only those involving the relation of the superior to the inferior. So we come down to justice and mercy, because every act of God's will that refers to creatures comes about either from pure grace, and thus pertains to mercy, which relieves the creature of his defects or needs, or comes about according to some note of debt at least on the supposition of a covenant, and thus pertains to justice. Hence it is said in Psalm 24, 10, "All the ways of the Lord are kindness and faithfulness," that is, operations tending to creatures, called "ways."

c. Mixed Attributes (**qq. 22–24**)

Saint Thomas goes on to discuss attributes which are not in intellect alone nor in will alone, but in intellect as moved by will. Such are the practical acts disposing or ordering freely that which is susceptible of being ordered or commanded. With respect to himself, God does not act by command or free ordination, because God's will bears on himself necessarily, since he is the highest good. Toward himself then he has a necessary love and supreme joy. God performs free practical acts with respect to creatures, ordering and disposing them. Since all creatures are subject to God as Supreme Lord, his providence and prudence, whose chief act is to command (IIaIIae, q. 47, a. 8), extends to all things. Thus Saint Thomas reduces everything he finds of practical acts in God, in which the ordination of intelligence and the efficacy of will concur, to the providence or prudence by which God disposes all things. He treats of this first in general (**q. 22**). Then (**q. 23**) he treats of special providence which efficaciously conducts the rational creature to his supernatural end. It is called special both as to the end to which it leads, which is supernatural beatitude, and as to persons, because not all but only some are brought to that end; and from mode, because it efficaciously leads to the end. This is called predestinating providence and is treated in **q. 23**. Scripture calls providence the Book of Life: **q. 24** explains this metaphor: a book is a written text which comes to the aid of memory. God's knowledge is similarly firm with respect to predestination, but also because a book is ordered to designate some to some office or function, but the elect are assigned the supreme function of enjoying God.

2. Divine Transitive Operation

Having explained the attributes which are purely immanent to God, Saint Thomas then explains the attribute of omnipotence, which is the executive principle whose act passes outside him (**q. 25**).

From all the things that have been said about the attributes which explain the most high and infinite perfection of

God in being and in operating, Saint Thomas concludes that supreme happiness belongs to God, since it is a state of the perfect gathering of all goods as known and enjoyed. He treats God's happiness in **q. 26.**

2. The Mystery of the Trinity

After considering the absolute perfections, which belong to God insofar as he is maximally one, we must consider those things within God which pertain to the distinction of the Persons and the mystery of the Trinity. Saint Thomas's discussion of them falls under three major headings, First, he considers things which must first be known as presupposed by the distinction of Persons, namely, processions and relations – he devotes two questions to these. Second, he considers the Persons themselves as constituted and distinct from one another, treating this first in a general way and then taking up each Person in particular – he devotes ten questions to these matters. Third, those things which follow on the comparison of the Persons, either within the Trinity or with respect to creatures – this in five questions.

a. Processions and Relations

The mystery of the Trinity consists in this that there are in God three really distinct persons within the highest unity of essence. The Catholic faith avoids two extreme and contrary heresies – from which yet others on this matter have arisen – the Sabellian and the Arian. Sabellius held that all the Persons are really one in themselves, and are distinguished only according to their different offices or external effects. In order to preserve the divinity of the Son Sabellius denies that he is the Son. Arius, on the contrary, distinguishes the Persons in God in such a way as to deny consubstantiality and unity of essence, and so, to preserve the Son as Son, he denied that he was God. To avoid both these heresies the Catholic faith holds that the distinction of Persons does not come about in what is absolute and essential, but according to real opposed relations. Among oppositions only relative opposites can be found without imperfection or division of nature in God, as Saint Thomas teaches in the *Disputed Question on the Power of God* (q. 7, a. 8, ad 4).[1] Other oppositions come about by removing something or by positing something in the substance to which they belong, and come about by way of negation and affirmation. Only relative opposition comes about by a reference tending to the opposite term without removing it, and thus it does not ground a division in being, but in respect. In God, everything is one save the opposition of relation.

If one wishes these relations to be real they must presuppose a real foundation. Without a real foundation, there are no real relations. A real relation or respect in God can only be grounded in some procession, or communicative origin of nature which is not divisive of it. Every other relation, grounded on any other basis, presupposes and does not cause distinct extremes. Origin or procession, however, produces the extremes and their relation. In God, antecedently to relations, there cannot be supposed distinct extremes between which the relation is exercised, because whatever is antecedent to relation is absolute and consequently not distinct but one. So only procession of origin can found real relations, not presupposing them as distinct prior to these relations, but made distinct by the relation which constitutes them: such relations are substantial and not accidental. Therefore he treats the divine processions as the foundations of relations within [the deity] in **q. 27**, and of the relations themselves in **q. 28**.

b. What Constitutes and Distinguishes Divine Persons
Having explained processions and relations, the second part of this treatise turns to the Persons themselves, whose constitution and distinction depends on relations or processions. Two general things come up for consideration now. First, that

---

1   The second reference given by John of St. Thomas is to an inauthentic work of Thomas's, viz. *In IV libros Sententiarum ad Hannibaldum* – a work by and not dedicated to Annibald.

which is common to all the Persons; second, that which is peculiar and proper to each.

The divine Persons in general. – There are four things to be considered which are common to all. First, the quiddity or definition or concept of person, in **q. 29**. Second, the division or plurality of Persons, in **q. 30**. Third, what follows on the division or plurality of Persons, and how the words 'plurality,' 'diversity,' or 'solitude' are used, in **q. 31**. Fourth, the knowability of Persons, and consequently their naming and discretion, which comes about through notions – in **q. 32**.

The divine Persons in particular. – First, the Person of the Father, in **q. 33**. Then the Person of the Son, with respect to his notion and function, in **q. 34**, and with respect to his image, in **q. 35**. Third, the Person of the Holy Spirit, both as spirit (**q. 36**), not taking spirit as opposed to the corporeal (for this is common to all Three Persons), but insofar as it means impulse and efficacy of will proceeding from the Father and Son who "breathe" him, both as the love of spirit (**q. 37**) and as the gift proceeding from or emitted by the giver, in **q. 38**.

c. Consequence of the Distinction of Persons and Their Comparison

Saint Thomas discusses five comparisons of the Persons. First, with reference to the essence which terminates them and the essential names whereby they are signified, in **q. 39**. Second, they are compared to the relations by which as personal forms they are constituted as persons, in **q. 40**. Third, they are compared to the notional acts according to which the Persons are originated or produced, in **q. 41**. Fourth, they are compared among themselves with respect to equality, grandeur and coeternity, and the like, in **q. 42**. Fifth, they are compared to creatures to whom the Persons are sent, not in the work of creation, which is common to all the Persons and belongs to them as one, but by the work of sanctification in which the Persons either visibly appear, as the Son through the incarnation, and the Holy Spirit through appearing, or as invisibly dwelling in the soul and sanctifying it: this sending or mission of the Persons is discussed in **q. 43**.

Created Nature
3. The Procession of Creatures from God
Next Saint Thomas begins to speak of God as causing, whereas up until now he had spoken of God as existing in himself. Saint Thomas discusses three things with respect to the procession of creatures from God.

First, what kind of cause can the first principle, who is God, be?

Second, the mode of causing, both with respect to the cause itself and with respect to the thing caused.

Third, the caused things in their variety.

a. The Procession of Creatures
1. God as First Cause
In **q. 44**, he shows that efficient, final and exemplar causality belong to the first principle. Matter is something caused by God and not a first cause, and thus material causality does not befit the first principle.

2. The Mode of Divine Causality
In **qq. 45–46** he discusses the mode pertaining to God as cause (**q. 45**), and the mode pertaining to creatures (**q. 46**). Here he treats God's causality only in the genus of efficient cause, since he will treat final causality fully in the First Part of the Second Part, when he treats the ultimate end of the rational creature. He has already discussed exemplar cause in **q. 45**. The mode of efficient cause in God is that he produces from nothing, because, as the first principle absolutely and in every genus, he presupposes nothing from which he produces, prime matter itself being created by God. Therefore he produces from non-matter – otherwise he would not produce matter itself – therefore from nothing, which is what creating means. The mode on the side of creatures is considered theologically insofar as he creates in time and not from all eternity: for this pertains to the declaration of the article of faith in which we confess that God created at the beginning of time.

3. Things Proceeding from God
Third, with respect to the things proceeding from God and

their diversity and distinction, Saint Thomas treats of them theologically insofar as they are integrated into the universe, which is the entire and total effect of God. Hence he first shows in general that diversity and inequality of things is given with the unity of the world, which is a unity of order, of both of which God is cause (**q. 47**).

b. The Distinction of Creatures
He now discusses in detail the kinds of things which make up the universe. As considered by the metaphysician, who considers their essential predicates, created things are divided by the ten categories. The theologian, however, considers the essences of creatures only insofar as they are effects of God and make up this universe; that is why he considers only the principle genera from which the universe is constituted as well as what causes inequality and hierarchy among the things in the universe. Those chief kinds are the corporeal, the spiritual, and mixed cases. As for inequality and hierarchy, they exist between the perfect and imperfect and defective, or generally between good and evil. Hence only these are explained here. It is the theologian's task alone to explain the distinction and multiplicity of creatures, none of which escape the jurisdiction of God who is the creator of the visible and invisible. Nor is there any distinction and multiplicity in creatures that would require two highest and first principles, as the Manicheans thought, who held that there is one good principle and another evil principle, and from one of them, who is God, they removed corporeal creatures, saying they are from the evil principle. So in order to show that the universe of creatures is from a single principle, that is, from God the creator, it was necessary to single out those kinds that some denied of God and attribute everything to him, both spiritual and corporeal, good and bad.

1. Good and Evil
With respect to the distinction of good and evil, we can set aside the good since it has already been treated (**q. 5**) and which no one doubts comes from God, and treat here only of

evil, which Saint Thomas didn't treat then but which is especially needed to explain the inequality and distinction of creatures. He discusses evil in general since evil in a special sense is moral and is treated n the Second Part. He takes up two things with regard to evil in general. First, the nature of evil and its division into the evil of fault and the evil of pain (**q. 48**) and second the cause of evil in general, in **q. 49**.

2. Spiritual, Corporeal, and Human
The division of creatures into spiritual and corporeal receives a very lengthy treatment because of the variety of natures covered. He treats first the purely spiritual nature, which the theologian calls angels, that is messengers of God, whereas the philosopher calls them intelligences. These are treated in **qq. 50–64**.

Second, he discusses purely corporeal nature which proceeded from God in the work of the six days in **qq. 65–74**.

Third, of the creature that is a mixture of the spiritual and corporeal, namely man, in **qq. 75–102**.

Although man has greater dignity than the purely corporeal, Saint Thomas speaks of the latter before the former both (i) because after the angels or with them purely corporeal nature was made – according to Scripture, "In the beginning God created heaven and earth" – and on the sixth day man was created and the theologian is especially required to explain the order of creatures and the way in which they proceed from God, and (ii) because that which is mixed or composed of both extremes is better known when knowledge of the extremes is had. Thus since man is composed of spirit and body he is rightly treated after spiritual and corporeal nature have been examined.

a. Purely Spiritual Creatures

The Treatise on the Angels
Saint Thomas considers spiritual creatures or angels under three principal headings. First, their substance or essence as such, abstracting from existence and production. Second, he

considers their natural existence, or creation. Third, their supernatural existence in grace and glory, and their opposites, namely sin and damnation.

The Essence of Angels. – Saint Thomas will discuss first the essence or substance of angels, then the properties consequent on it, namely, intellect, will, and their operations. He considers the nature or substance both in itself and by comparison with bodies (**q. 50**). Angels are compared both to the bodies which they assume when they appear, although they are not naturally united to them, and to the bodies to whom they are locally present by virtual quantity and to the bodies they move and in which they are moved, because what exists in place is mutable and can only be treated with local motion. The comparison of the angels with the bodies they assume and with which they are not naturally united is found in **q. 51**. The comparison with bodies taken as places of their presence is found in **q. 52**. Motion with respect to such place is discussed in **q. 53**.

The Properties of Angels. – Saint Thomas treats of intellect first and then of will, and with respect to intellect, he discusses four things. First, their knowing power of angels, in **q. 54**. Second, the means through which their knowledge comes about, namely, angelic species, in **q. 55**. Third, the objects on which angelic knowledge bears, which are immaterial and spiritual, in **q. 56**. The angel also knows corporeal things and those manifested corporeally, such as thoughts of the heart which are manifested through bodily signs, or by miracles, such as the mysteries of grace, in **q. 57**. Fourth, he considers the mode of knowing which is non-discursive, without composition and the like, in **q. 58**. As for the angelic will, he treats first the power of free will, in **q. 59**, and then as a natural act and as free, in **q. 60**.

Creation of Angels. – After considering the essence of the angel, we must consider their being brought into existence, their creation, and the circumstances of this creation, as to time and place, in **q. 61**.

Supernatural Being of Angels – Third and last the supernatural existence to which the angel is raised and from which the sinning angels fell. All this is discussed in **q. 62**. The special difficulties relative to merit, happiness, and grace arise in the case of man as well as the angels, and they are considered later in the First Part of the Second Part, qq. 109–114. Here he goes on to the opposite of grace which is sin, and how and when it can come about, in **q. 63**. Next he treats the opposite of glory, which is damnation or the punishment of sinners, both with respect to the darkening of intellect and the obstinacy of will as well as the sorrow in the captivity of fire, in **q. 64**.

b. Purely Corporeal Creatures

Bodily Creatures and the Work of the Six Days
After the consideration of angelic nature, which is purely spiritual, we must inquire into the other kind of creature proceeding from God, that which is purely corporeal. Saint Thomas determines the order in which such creatures should be studied in a theological manner, that is, this process is treated insofar as it pertains to faith, as given in the revelation of Sacred Scripture. Therefore this treatise is governed by the way the production of corporeal creatures is made known in Scriptural revelation. Scripture tells us of four kinds of divine works by which the whole world has been brought to perfection: the work of creation; the work of distinction; the work of adorning; and the work of completion or consummation. Although God could have produced this perfection and completion by creation alone, as he made the angels, he conforms his action to the natures of things. Therefore he creates or brings from nothing those things which could come into being in no other way, celestial bodies and the elements. As for those creatures that can come into being by generation, needing to be 'educed' from the potency of a subject, those he

produced by generation from a subject. Moreover, not only the power of the one creating should be shown in the first formation of things but also the wisdom of the one ordering, as well as the imperfection and dependence of the things created. This is most manifestly shown by the wise ordering of the universe and the transition of bodies from an imperfect to a perfect state. Thus, after having created, that is, drawn from nothing, the first bodies, including the substantial differences of bodies – for he is said to have created heaven and earth, which are substantially distinct bodies – God begins the work of distinction or separation by means of accidental changes, such as through the movement of light the division of night from day; by the segregation of the waters; the division of the firmament of clouds from inferior waters; by the separation of the waters, the manifesting of earth; and so forth.

The third phase of the creative work was one of furnishing or adorning, as certain mixed and living bodies are added from the elements, birds of the air, fish of the sea, the beasts of the earth, and by the additional power of the heavenly bodies this adornment of the lower is affected.

The work of completion or consummation does not consist of the production of new species by God but the continuing governance of new individuals which perpetuate the species.

This then is the order that Saint Thomas follows and the plan of his treatise on God's production of the corporeal world: First, he shows in general and universally that corporeal creatures proceed from God, not from the angels, in **q. 65**. He then treats in detail each of the single works.

First, the work of creation as other than the work of distinction, showing that some bodies are brought about by creation and why they were given distinct substantial forms, whereas accidental forms are acquired later. This is the subject of **q. 66**.

Second, he treats the work of distinguishing which in the course of three days was accomplished in three ways. *On the first day* God separated light and darkness, which pertains to celestial bodies: Saint Thomas treats the production of light in **q. 67**. *On the second day* God divided air and water, producing the upper waters, that is, the clouds, and the lower waters, the seas, by means of the firmament, that is, in the second region of air in which the waters of the clouds are held and, as it were, bound lest they fall at once upon the earth. The waters do not rise to the firmament of the stars so as to make necessary their separation from what is below, in **q. 68**. *On the third day* there is the separation for water and earth by the segregation of the waters and the appearance of the land with the seeds and plants which adorn it, in **q. 69**.

The furnishing of the corporeal world, both the celestial and elemental bodies, is accomplished in the course of three days. *On the fourth day* the heavens were adorned with lights endowed with a special power for the production of things, on which is impressed a movement which divides time into months and days, as if composed of the wheels of a clock, in **q. 70**. *On the fifth day* air and water were furnished, producing the fish of the sea and the birds of the air, in **q. 71**. *On the sixth day* the earth is furnished with living things and finally with man as the lord and ruler of it, in **q. 72**.

The work of completion or consummation being accomplished, *on the seventh day* God rested, **q. 73**. In order to complete this doctrine, Saint Thomas treats generally of God at work in the seven days and solves certain difficulties concerning them, in. **q. 74**.

c. Creatures Composed of Body and Spirit

The Treatise on Man

Having considered purely spiritual creatures and purely corporeal creatures, there remains to consider the creature composed of the spiritual and corporeal, namely, man, the microcosm being treated after the macrocosm, as it were. Just as in the macrocosm corporeal creatures are bodies and angels are spirits which minister to and move but do not inform bodies, so in the microcosm that is man there is spirit, that is the soul that informs, and body, which is given life and ruled by spirit. The theologian however does not consider the nature of man save on the part of the soul, although he considers body as that to which soul is related and generally as an effect of God: later (**q. 91**) he treats of the production of the human body. But it is the task of the philosopher, not of the theologian, to consider the body as mobile being and corruptible. Therefore the theologian is chiefly concerned with the intellectual nature of the soul and the way in which it is specially ordered to God.

Like that on the angels, the treatise on man comprises two parts. First, the nature of man as such; second, the production of man by God.

1. The Nature of Man (**qq. 75–89**)

Fifteen questions are devoted to the nature of man; his production occupies thirteen (**qq. 90–102**). As for the nature of man with especial attention to soul, which is the theologian's chief interest, Saint Thomas considers the soul's essence, powers and operations, just as he did with the angel.

The Essence of Soul comprises two discussions. First, the substance absolutely and in itself in **q. 75**. Then it is considered with reference to the body to which it is united as its form, in which it differs from the substances which are totally separate, in **q. 76**. He does not treat of the status of soul as separated from the body here, but below, after he has treated the operations of the soul, because that status greatly affects the soul's mode of operating without dependence on body.

The Powers of the Soul. – He considers them first in general (**q. 77**) and then in particular. And because the principal powers are intellect and will, which the sense powers serve, he first treats the external and internal sense powers which precede and serve the intellectual powers in **q. 78**. He treats of the intellectual powers in **q. 79**. And, because appetite follows on intellectual knowledge, he treats man's appetitive power, first in general and as such (**q. 80**), then specifically sense appetite which serves and is presupposed by the rational (**q. 81**), next the will (**q. 82**), and because indifference and liberty are found in will, insofar as it is moved by an indifferent judgment, free will is discussed in **q. 83**.

Operations of the soul. – He first considers the operations of the soul as united to body, then those of the separated soul; the operations of will and the habits, since they are moral and have the note of virtue or vice, will be treated in the First Part of the Second Part, as will the habits of intellect which are virtues, namely, wisdom and prudence and so on. Saint Thomas treats the acts of understanding by distinguishing them according to the objects known. There is a threefold difference of objects: some are below the intellectual, such as bodies; then there is the soul itself; third are the things above it, namely intelligences and God. In knowing bodies, or sensible essences which are more connatural to us in this state, there are three things to be considered. First, the means of knowing, which are species as they depend on phantasms and are drawn from things, in **q. 84**. Second, the order and manner of knowing. By order is meant the way some things are prior, and others posterior, and things are known in greater or lesser universality. By mode is meant knowing by composing and dividing, discursively, and the like, all discussed in **q. 85**. Third, he considers the things themselves known and the objects to which the intellect can extend, for example, to singulars, future events, infinities, and so on; all this in **q. 86**. He then considers how it [soul] knows itself and the things within it, in **q. 87**; and how it knows angels and God, which are above it, in **q. 88**. Finally he considers how soul in a state of separation knows all these things, in **q. 89**. And that ends the treatise of man with respect to his soul.

2. The Production of Man (**qq. 90–102**)

The production of man is treated by Saint Thomas as a theologian does, that is, as it is made known in Scripture. He considers four things which Scripture tells us of the first production of man. First, it tells of the production itself: "Let us make man to our image and likeness; And God created man. "(Genesis 1, 26, 27) Second, it states his end, "to have dominion." (Genesis 1, 26) Third, the condition in which man was constituted, because God made him righteous and without sin in a state of innocence. Fourth, it states the place in which God placed man, "And the Lord God took man and put him into the paradise of pleasure, to dress it and to keep it." (Genesis 2, 15) Whatever Saint Thomas says of the production of man is summed up in these four.

The production itself occupies three questions. First the production of the soul, in **q. 90**; then the production of the human body, in **q. 91**; and then the production of the adjunct body, that is, the body of the woman, which is joined to him for the generation of life and to submit to him, in **q. 92**.

As for the end of man, since he is created in the image and likeness of God, Saint Thomas asks what is meant by image and likeness, in **q. 93**.

As for man's first state, he treats that on the part of the soul and on the part of the body. For the intellect, this meant the fullness of knowledge and science (**q. 94**); for the will, rectitude of grace and original justice (**q. 95**); in the use of this justice man had dominion over all lesser creatures (**q. 96**). As for the body, Saint Thomas asks about the conservation of the individual and propagation through generation. Thus he considers the body's immortality due to this original state of man, not however that of future glory when the body will become spiritual, that is, perfectly subject to spirit. In the state of innocence the body remained an "animal body" (1 Corinthians 15, 44), that is, needing to nourish itself and was subject to change, although by the Providence of God from without, and the fruit of the tree of life, it was made immune to death; this is treated in **q. 97**. As for the body in the state of innocence with respect to generation, he considers it both with respect to the generating principle – because in the common way generation would come about through intercourse,

though not with the bestial concupiscence it has now (**q. 98**) –
and with respect to the offspring generated, first as to its body
and the perfection of it as generated (**q. 99**) and then as to its
soul, with respect to original justice, which is transmitted to
the child (**q. 100**) and whether the child has knowledge or the
use of reason (**q. 101**).

Finally, as to where man was placed when he was first
made, namely paradise, he treats in **q. 102**.

c. The Governance of Creatures

After completing the consideration of the procession of creatures from God, there remains their governance and adminis-
tration, which God continuously operates, according to John
5, 17: "My Father works even until now, and I work."

God governs the world by bringing about some things
immediately and others by the mediation of secondary causes; Augustine says in *On the Trinity* (III, 4) that grosser bodies
are ruled by the more subtle ones and all bodies by the rational soul; the sinner's spirit by the just spirit, and the just spirit
by God. Consequently a complete study of the divine governance will include: first, God's immediate governance of the
creature; second, his mediated governance, whereby one
thing is acted on by another.

1. God's Immediate Governance

Under this heading is considered God's immediate governance of creatures, both in itself and in its effects. The first is
discussed in **q. 103**. He considers the effects of immediate
governance, both what the continuation or conservation of
things in existence is, and the concursive aid for acting. Of the
conservation in existence and the complete dependence of
creatures on God in order to exist, and its opposite, namely,
annihilation, should the conservation by God be suspended,
he speaks in **q. 104**. Of God's concourse in their acting, both
generally with every created thing and specially with intellect
and will, on which powers alone God penetrates and acts,
and miraculously in works exceeding their ordinary mode of
operating. He speaks of the kinds of miracle in **q. 105**.

2. God's Mediated Governance

As for God's governance when one creature acts on another, Saint Thomas observes that any change or action comes about in three ways because of the three kinds of creature previously distinguished, namely, the spiritual or angelic, the purely corporeal insofar as one body acts on another, and man, who is made up of the corporeal and spiritual.

a. Angels

An angel can act on and change another angel, or a corporeal creature, or man. One angel can act on another either in the hierarchical action of the superior on the inferior, or by an action common to all, which is the angelic word. The first sort of action is treated in **q. 106** and is called illumination, under which is included purgation, which removes lack of knowledge of the truth, and illumination itself, which shows the truth in a manner proportionate to the capacity of the inferior, and thus strengthens his light; and finally perfection, which elevates the inferior to a superior mode of knowing, and thus also inflames his will.

Of the action that is simple speech, when the thought of one angel which was morally hidden from another is related to him and thus is no longer hidden to him, he treats in **q. 107**.

There is necessarily an order among the higher and lower angels and a primacy which constitutes the angelic hierarchy.

Among the good angels this action is illuminating and perfective (**q. 108**). As for the bad angels, they are incapable of supernatural illumination and perfection, since they are devoid of grace, but retain only a natural primacy and direction, as is said in **q. 109**. Priority or hierarchy in the angels is based on greater and lesser universality of knowledge which determines the differences in influence and governance.

The first hierarchy. – This hierarchy comprises three choirs and can be understood in terms of three things. Some angels consider things and order them insofar as they proceed from the first principle who is God, and this belongs to the first hierarchy by which things are ordered and disposed according to what proceeds immediately from God and as decreed by him. The Seraphim inflame the will, the Cherubim illumine the intellects of all intellectual creatures and can thus govern them as being above them. The powers of intellect and will, because they are most universal, can be moved immediately only by God. Finally, Thrones show and exercise the judgments and decrees of God as they proceed immediately from God. These constitute the first hierarchy and can be likened to the men who make up the entourage of a king, assisting him in what he himself does as ministers and counselors.

Second hierarchy. – Other angels know and govern events insofar as they proceed from universal created causes, and they make up the second hierarchy also composed of three choirs. Dominations preside and direct the good angels; Powers coerce the bad angels; Virtues move the heavens. The second hierarchy can be likened to those who are charged by a king to govern provinces.

Third hierarchy. – Other angels know things as they proceed from particular created causes and their immediate principles. The three choirs that make up this hierarchy are executive with respect to the things that come about in this world by the order of God. They are distinguished according to the importance of the missions assigned them. They are to God as agents to a king, exercising his power; they are lesser functionaries. The levels in this hierarchy are based on the dignity or gravity of the task assigned.[2]

Having discussed how the angel acts on the purely spiritual creature, he goes on to treat the way the angel governs and acts on the purely corporeal creature. Body is naturally subject to spirit and is fittingly ruled by it, not as if the angel

2 Lavaud notes the following: "If faith teaches us that there is a hierarchy among the angels, it tells us nothing of the nature of this hierarchy or the number of orders that make it up. Saint Augustine, while proclaiming his firm faith in the existence of Thrones, Dominations, Principalities and Powers, confesses his ignorance of their distinctive properties. Different Fathers give different explanations of the hierarchies and orders of the angels. Saint Thomas follows the lead of Pseudo-Denis the Areopagite."

changes it as to form, since the angel does not have generative and seminal power over bodies, let alone creative. But he changes them according to locomotion, which is more perfect and general in that it can apply to many things, and thus by applying the active to the passive, the angel can bring about many marvelous things, as is shown in **q. 110.**

As for the way in which the angel can change and govern man, there are two things to take up. First, what they can do by their natural power, and second, what they can do by way of God's mission or permission. By their own power they can act on man's intellect by illuminating it as they do another angel's, but not by an infusion of light within the intellect, that being proper to the creator. They can move the will by way of proposing an object to it, not by acting within it. They can directly alter imagination and sense, by moving locally the bodily factors involved in sensation (**q. 111**).

As for what angels on a mission from God do to the good or the evil by his permission, two things are shown. First, that missions are assigned to angels. Second, the effect of such a mission. Mission itself is discussed in **q. 112**, where he shows that all angels can be sent, though in different ways, for the higher preside and direct, and these are properly said to assist God in his governance. Others have the mission of executing, and are called ministers in some external ministry, though they also assist God in the sense of contemplating him in the beatific vision. Hence neither the whole of the first hierarchy nor the first order of the second hierarchy, namely Dominations, have the mission of executing.

The effect of such missions or permissions on the part of the good angels with respect to man is to be men's guardians, both singly and universally with respect to a kingdom or province. God assigns this guardianship to Archangels and also to Principalities. There can also be conflict and contrariety among the angels, not because their wills are contrary the one to the other, but because of the things whose guardian they are (**q. 113**). The bad angels receive permission to tempt men and to attack them (**q. 114**).

b. Purely Corporeal Creatures

The changing and governance by means of which one bodily creature acts on another, both the lower bodies which act through seminal reasons and heavenly bodies which act by locomotion and light and other higher influences derived from the motion of the angel, are treated in **q. 115**. Since bodies act with necessity, and an ordered series of bodily causes has an immutable and necessary disposition, which some call fate, he discusses fate in **q. 116**, showing that fate is not the result of the movement of heavenly bodies but God's providence, which is infallible and universal, governs all the corporeal effects, including the contingent. As it is in God, this is called governance or active providence. This disposition and ordering by God as it is received in created causes is called fate, as something spoken or uttered by God, which cannot be changed.

c. Man

Of man's governance of and causality on creatures, Saint Thomas notes that man can both change some things outside himself and things within himself. He acts outside himself in two ways: first, by his intellectual power and by executing locomotion as does the angel; second, by the seminal power as do other bodies, something angels do not have. With respect to the first, which pertains to illumining and teaching and moving, Saint Thomas discusses it in **q. 117**. The manner of changing by seminal reason and propagating, when a soul does not proceed from the soul of the generator, but comes about by God's creating it, is discussed in **q. 118**. The change a man brings about within himself is exemplified by his nourishing himself, and so he treats nourishment in **q. 119**.

And that ends the First Part.

Detailed Outline of
The First Part of the Second Part

The First Part of the Second Part

The Order and Connections of Its Treatises

The End of Man and Human Acts

After Saint Thomas has considered God in himself and as the efficient cause of creatures in the First Part, in the second part he turns to God as the final cause to be attained by the creature. But God is attainable only through intellect and will, that is, by knowledge and love, because other activities, not being spiritual, cannot attain him. This means that only the intellectual creature is capable of attaining God. Setting aside the angelic creature, whose happiness as well as its attainability were discussed in the First Part, there remains to study God as the end attainable by human acts. These are more easily known by us than angelic ones and more necessary to know since it is by them that we either arrive at God by way of virtue or recede from him because of vice and sin. These are called moral acts because they are human, and look to human customs or mores which distinguish man from brute.

In the First Part of the Second Part, two chief things are treated. First, the end of man as man. Second, moral or voluntary acts in general, and their principles, through which we tend to this end.

1. Man's Ultimate End

Saint Thomas finds the note of ultimate end chiefly in God, both because only God can be an ultimate or supreme end and because when the ultimate end is known it is easy to find the intermediate or non-ultimate ends. Saint Thomas considers three principal formalities in the ultimate end as it pertains to morality and is attainable through moral acts. First, how God is the human end and attainable in a human way, since this is the essence of morality. Second, how all other ends are subordinate to it, because it is first and supreme. Third, that there is nothing beyond it to be desired, because it is ultimate, satisfying and completing every perfection of our intellectual nature; it is our happiness and felicity. Thomas treats the first two notes of the ultimate end in q. 1, and the third – that it constitutes our happiness – in the four succeeding questions.

In **q. 1**, he takes up the notion of ultimate end *as human*, that is, as finalizing man not because he is moved by it but because he moves himself toward it and acts for the sake of it by discovering and referring means to it. The proximate end or object also specifies human acts as investing the object with the note of that toward which one moves himself.

Saint Thomas locates the essence of the *ultimate* end in this that it subordinates all other things to it as their end and thus must be one if ultimate in this way, since otherwise it would not subordinate all things to itself nor would all things be done for its sake.

He goes on to treat the ultimate end according to the third formality, as invested with the note of *happiness* and the ultimate perfecting felicity, satisfying the rational creature just because it is ultimate, leaving nothing outside itself to be desired.

There are three things to be considered about happiness: the state of happiness; what happiness requires; and whether or not it can be achieved.

First, Saint Thomas considers happiness itself objectively, that is, with respect to that in which it is found; and then formally, that is, with respect to the act by which it is attained – these are the *finis qui* (which) and the *finis quo* (by which). The end taken objectively means that thing which is the end; whereas the end taken formally means the possession or attainment of the end. Saint Thomas considers happiness itself to be the end taken objectively, both negatively by showing that in which it could not consist, that is, by showing it could not be any creature, and positively, by showing it is God (q. 2) who, since he is the most universal good, alone can fulfill the universal capacity of intellect and will. Saint Thomas considers happiness taken formally, that is, as the *finis quo*, in q. 3, showing that it resides in the intellectual part, not in will, but in intellect, particularly speculative intellect, since a thing must be first grasped and held before the will can enjoy it. The grasping and holding of God comes about through intellect, and thus in its operation the ultimate end is attained.

He treats happiness as a state in q. 4, showing what must concur for happiness to be had – on the side of the intellect, the vision or comprehension and possession of God, on the side of will, the highest delight and joy and indefectible rectitude. On the part of the body which is rendered immortal and completely perfect and adorned with the gifts of glory. As for external goods, he shows that they are in no way required; as for friends, that there is need of fitting society.

Finally, in q. 5, he considers the attainability of such happiness, and the fact that it cannot be lost once had, and that it cannot be attained in this life by any natural action or created thing but only if God supernaturally elevates the soul in order that it might see him clearly.

Having explained the notion of the human end as ultimate and beatifying, Saint Thomas must treat of the *moral acts* by which man attains or fails to attain it – that is the second principal thing studied in this treatise. Since the exact knowledge of moral activities requires that they be treated not only in general but also in their particular matters, he treats the former in the First Part of the Second Part and the latter in the Second Part of the Second Part.

Saint Thomas's general treatment comprises two principal treatises. First, human acts as such; second, their principles. And since the principles of a thing are sought through its causes, that is, the final, efficient, material, and formal, and he has treated of the final cause of human acts in the five preceding questions, he must take up the matter on which such acts bear. As for their form, that is, what specifies them, this will be postponed to the Second Part of the Second Part, where each specific kind of human act is treated. As for the efficient cause, which is the soul and its powers, that has already been treated in the First Part when soul was discussed. So there remains to discuss in the First Part of the Second Part only the moral principles which are added to the powers in human acts, whether intrinsic, that is, the habits of virtues and vices, or extrinsic, coming to them from an external principal, that is, law and grace.

2. Properly Human Acts

Saint Thomas devotes forty-three questions to the discussion of human or moral acts (**qq. 6–48**). There are two kinds of human or moral acts: first, those that are such by their nature, because they are acts of the rational and spiritual powers, to the objects of which the human agent properly tends. He treats these in **qq. 6–21**. Second, there are other acts which are moral only by way of participation and as caused by the first kind. They are common to men and brutes just as are the powers from which they proceed; they are the acts of the sense appetites and are called passions, which are also found in brutes. But because man can direct the passions by his reason, according to Genesis 4, 7: "But the lust thereof shall be under thee, and thou shalt have dominion over it," the passions participate in morality insofar as they are ruled and moved by reason. He treats these from **qq. 22–48**.

a. In General
1. Essentially Moral Acts

With regard to the elicited acts of the rational powers, he has already sufficiently treated the purely speculative acts of knowledge in the First Part, q. 84. Here he considers only moral acts by which man tends to the end and means. Such acts are necessarily voluntary because they look to the end and move the other powers to their ends. But because will cannot be its own rule by which it is directed and tends to the appropriate end, will would often be defective if it desired only whatever it wanted, usurping the role of reason. Human acts, insofar as they seek the end as desirable, are voluntary, but insofar as they seek it as right and obligatory, they must be regulated. It is reason that rules man because it is peculiar to man to live according to reason. Therefore, in order to explain human and moral acts, Saint Thomas first takes up the notion of the voluntary, which is, as it were, material to human acts (qq. 6–17). Then he considers what regulation is which is formal to morality in q. 18 where he takes up goodness and badness which follow from regulation by or deviation from the rule.

a. Acts Peculiar to Man
1. The Voluntary
Saint Thomas first considers the notion of the voluntary act and then its various kinds.

On the first point, both the essence and the accidents of the voluntary are considered. Its substance or essence is revealed by noting that the voluntary act has its principle within and requires knowledge of the end. The impediments to the voluntary are then taken up, and they are either external, such as violence and fear, or involve ignorance or passion, which impede or diminish knowledge. All this is in q. 6. The accidents of the voluntary, circumstances and their number, are discussed in q. 7.

Second, he turns to the various voluntary acts. A first distinction is that between elicited and commanded acts. The commanded act always presupposes a prior act by which it is commanded, and therefore cannot bear immediately on the end, but only on things ordered to the end. The elicited act can concern either end or means. The second distinction is based on the acts of will, some of which concern the end, others the means. Three acts are concerned with the end, two respecting it absolutely, *wish* or simple volition, and *enjoyment*, by which will rests or takes pleasure in the end willed. The third concerns end as achievable by certain means, namely, *intention*.

a. Acts of Will Bearing on the End

The first of these, will (*voluntas*) is discussed in **q. 8.** It is not now a matter of will as a power but rather of its act of simple volition. [*Voluntas* is used to signify both the will and this first act of the will.] Before treating the second such will-act, namely, enjoyment, Saint Thomas devotes two questions to asking what moves the will. The Holy Doctor does this because simple volition is the first act of will, and here will cannot be moved by anything willed before; therefore the origination and cause of this first act is obscure and hidden. In other acts the cause and origin is manifest in that later acts are dependent on prior acts; for example, will chooses means because it intends the end, and it intends the end because it loves it. But the first love cannot be caused by any prior act. That is why Saint Thomas specially inquires into its cause or origin. It has to come from outside, and that seems contrary to the notion of the voluntary.

Two things have to be taken up with respect to this cause. First, he asks what the moving principle of the first act of will is, both on the side of the object proposed, which specifies the act, and on the side of its efficient cause. The will in its first act cannot be the efficient cause of its own activity since no prior act is presupposed by which its potentiality might be actuated. So it must be moved by an external agent which can only be God. Of this moving principle he treats in **q. 9.**

Second, he asks whether the will is moved necessarily or freely by its specifying object, by the inclination of inferior appetite, and by the external cause God. God acts infallibly and as a universal cause and therefore does not impose necessity or take away freedom. On this, see **q. 10.**

Having discussed the first act of will bearing on the end, he goes on to another act which bears on the end absolutely, namely, enjoyment. This is not the perfect enjoyment that comes from the real attainment and possession of the end, but an imperfect one which follows on the initial love which finds the end pleasant when it is had only intentionally. The end begins to move as what is first in intention. That is why Saint Thomas treats enjoyment immediately after the will's simple act of volition. Although perfect and consummate enjoyment is the last of the acts of will (all motion ceases once the end is attained), still the inchoate rest in the thing loved, when it is first had intentionally through love, follows immediately on the first simple act of will. Enjoyment is treated in **q. 11**.

The third act of will that bears on the end is not absolute but comparative, for after the will wills something such that it adheres to and takes pleasure in it, we seek its accomplishment so as not only to love but to intend, that is, to bend ourselves to acquiring the thing. Thus we are moved from imperfect and intentional enjoyment toward perfect and fulfilled enjoyment. This act of intention is such that by it we do not simply love the end as such, but also look for the ways and means by which it can be arrived at. Of this act and its object, which is not only the ultimate end but any end, he treats in **q. 12**. These three, simple volition, enjoyment, and intention, are all the acts of the will that in the order of intention bear on the end.

b. Acts of Will Bearing on the Means

After the foregoing acts, the will relates to the means which follow on the intention of the end, and the order of execution begins. The will is moved by the means in two ways. First, to desire them, holding them affectively. Second, to search for the means to achieve them and effectively realize them.

Choice is required if they are to be present effectively in the will, since by choosing will determines itself to pursue effectively some determinate means. Since this is the chief act of will as looking to the means and comes before the executive acts, he treats of *choice* in **q. 13**. But just as the simple act of volition requires a special cause originating it, so choice requires some cause which brings it about immediately. And since the first motive, and the reason for willing, is the intended end, out of love for it the will is inclined to accept the means of pursuing it. But this is not a sufficient motive to determine it with respect to one means as opposed to another, especially when many present themselves. Therefore some inference and determination of the fittingness of means to end must be made. This determination is made by *counsel* which includes inquiry or inference and determination of judgment. Judgment about things to be desired arises chiefly from experience and assent *(consensus)*, thanks to which what is considered pleases so that one adheres to it because of its pleasantness. This adherence or consent pertains to will as it applies itself to taking pleasure in the means, similar to enjoyment of the end. Thus choice follows on the intellectual act of counsel as a cause, treated in **q. 14**, and consent on the will's enjoyment; this is treated in **q. 15**. Choice adds to consent the determination of the means chosen, because it can sometimes happen that several of the means arrived at through counsel please, each bringing about the act of consent, and only afterward is will determined to one among them, and in this choice is perfected.

After choice, by which will is moved toward the means so that they might be affectively held, the will begins to realize and execute the means. Two acts are involved here. For execution, directing is first required, intellect ordering that something should be done, since execution should be rational and ordered, and command fulfills this function. Moreover, the will must cause other powers to execute their acts not only in an orderly fashion but also voluntarily insofar as they come under the sway of will. This application of will to the other powers causing them to act is called *use*. Saint Thomas treats use first, although in exterior matters command precedes use, both because use is the act of will itself whereas command is the act of reason, and the order of doctrine requires that he first treat all the acts of will. Another reason is that use is more universal than command, because some instance of use precedes command, namely that whereby will applies the intellect to those things required for choice, but the use which applies the executive powers follows on command. He treats of use in **q. 16** and of command in **q. 17**.

c. Summary

There are thus twelve distinct acts from the grasp of the end to its execution. First, on the part of intellect there is the grasp of the end or good. Second, on the part of will there is the simple act of volition bearing on the end. Third, there is the imperfect enjoyment of the end as grasped intentionally.

Fourth, there is intention which is already an act relating end to means. All these acts belong to the order of intention. Then he turns to the willing of the means. Fifth, will moves intellect to take counsel, and this is a certain use prior to choice. Sixth, there is counsel on the part of intellect. Seventh, there is consent on the part of the will with respect to the means turned up by counsel. Eighth, choice which selects the means. All these belong to the order of execution in the will. Ninth, there is the realizing of the means, the precept or command to act. Tenth, the use of will applying the other powers in order to execute. Eleventh, the execution of the act. Twelfth, the attainment of the end and perfect enjoyment. All these belong to the bringing about of the effect.

2. On Morality

Having considered voluntary acts as such which are, as it were, the material governed by morality, there remains to consider them with respect to their morality, that is, as they are formally ruled and ordered by reason. Since it is proper to man to live according to reason, the will should bear on the desirable as regulated by the rules of reason. That is what makes it moral, that is, rational or governed by the rule of reason. It pertains to reason to impose and to possess the moral.

Therefore, Saint Thomas discusses two things concerning formal morality thanks to which acts are said to be good or bad. First, the moral as such (**through q. 20**); second, its properties (**q. 21**).

a. The Moral as Such

Saint Thomas teaches that morality as such is found in acts proportioned to the will as it bears on the object, either absolutely or in the way one causes another, as when from the end that is willed one tends toward the means. That moving and prior act is called the interior act, and the moved act is called exterior, because the will goes beyond the first act and moves the other. Sometimes it is called the exterior act not only because it is without and the act of another power but because it pertains to another power and is outside the moving power, as sensible acts are called exterior with respect to spiritual acts by which they are directed. Thus it is that Saint Thomas discusses three aspects of moral acts: first, morality absolutely and in general; second, the morality of interior or commanding acts; third, the morality of external acts.

With respect to the first, Saint Thomas treats the ways in which acts participate in morality. Over and above natural goodness (which is presupposed materially to the moral), there is goodness or evil as such, that is, the full conformity to the rule or falling away from it, which can come about either in the species of the act or in the individual act, both of which are governed by reason. Objects are the principles of the species of acts, and so it is that morality properly speaking derives from objects. Circumstances are required for the individuation of acts, the chief of which is the end, which is not a simple circumstance, but itself a moving cause on which goodness of the exterior or moved act depends as on a prime mover. In the order of moving, the end is more formal and actual, although in the order of specification the object is more formal. Saint Thomas shows that there are four ways in which goodness or badness pertains to acts. First, there is natural goodness, which is materially presupposed by the moral. Second, there is the species of morality drawn from the object. Third, morality depends on the end as on the first moving cause in the order of intention. Fourth, it depends on other circumstances as on the accidents of morality, though it sometimes happens that a defect in a circumstance leads to the defect in the type or species of act, thus altering the object. If the object, insofar as it is an object, does not affect the note of conformity or non-conformity with reason, it is said to be morally indifferent with respect to object or species (q. 18).

Saint Thomas goes on to discuss the morality of interior acts, the acts which are prior to and move others. Because the will is moved by the end, such acts are said to have the end for their object, and are called willing (*voluntas*), because volition or simple willing bears on the end. But as was pointed out earlier in treating of willing or simple volition as such, we must ask what caused it, since it is the first act of will; so now in treating of the morality of interior or primary acts we must seek the principle or cause of their regulation and morality.

Such acts do not have this by participation in something prior since they are first; they can only derive it from their object, which is the end. Such an object derives its moral goodness from dependence on governing law and on the divine legislator or the divine will, and from reason proposing or applying, according to the dictate of conscience. Thus it is necessary to treat of its conformity with a correct or erroneous conscience, with the divine will, with law, and so forth (q. 19).

With respect to the morality of external acts, that is, those which are caused and commanded by other acts prior to them, Saint Thomas holds that they not only depend on their proper object and circumstances, but also on the prior act and intention of the end by which they are commanded and moved. Therefore the morality they have from their proper object is not due to some other act, but is solely dependent on the ruling law and on the regulated object. But the morality they have from the end is by way of participation in the prior act of intention which tends toward the end and lends its goodness to the commanded acts. With respect to the goodness derived from the end, the moral goodness of internal and external acts is the same. The proper goodness of the commanded acts, that is, what they have from their proper object, is distinct from that which they have from the end and from the commanding act (q. 20).

b. The Properties of Morality

Having explained the notion of morality in interior and external acts, he turns now to the properties of morality, which are three, rightness and sin, being worthy of praise or blame, merit and demerit, all of which he treats in q. 21.

b. Imperfectly Moral Acts (Acts Common to Men and Animals)

After Saint Thomas explains the acts which are properly human, because they belong to intellect and will, he next treats of acts which are human by way of participation and belong to sense appetite which is common to men and brutes, but in man is governable by reason. These acts are called passions because they are accompanied by a certain bodily change. Saint Thomas, in his usual manner, treats of them first in general and then specifically.

1. The Passions
a. General Consideration

This involves four things. First, what passion is in general; second, the types of passion; third, their moral goodness or badness; fourth, the order among the passions.

First, then, Saint Thomas asks how passions can pertain to the soul, not only passions commonly so called, which are found in the spiritual powers as well, but those properly so called, that is, involving a bodily change, as in the senses and appetite (q. 22).

Second, he divides the passions according to a threefold principle. First, on the basis of the diverse powers; second, on the part of contrary objects; third, on the part of the distinct mode and application of the object, such as absent and present. In the first way, the quasi-general passions of the irascible and concupiscible differ, such as wrath and love, hope and joy. In the second way, passions of the same power are distinguished on the part of contrary objects, such as fear and boldness, love and hate, joy and sadness. Finally, in the third way, passions are distinguished by their distinct grasp of the object as applied. For example, fear turns on an absent evil but sadness on a present one, desire on a future thing, enjoyment a present, because by the different application and grasp of the object they are moved differently (he treats this in q. 23). Gathering them all together, he finds that there are eleven passions, six in the concupiscible (love and hate, which look to good and evil absolutely; desire and flight which look to an absent good or evil; delight and sadness, which look to a present good or evil.) There are five in the irascible (hope and despair with respect to the possible or impossible; fear and boldness which look to an evil which can be conquered or not; wrath which looks to a present imminent evil).

Third, the interconnection of the passions. Saint Thomas considers that they can be ranked as prior and posterior in two ways. First, on the part of the powers, as the concupiscible precedes the irascible absolutely speaking, for a man is moved first by the absolute good and then by a difficult one. Second, in the same power, insofar as passions that regard the good precede those which regard evil, as in the concupiscible love precedes hate, and in the irascible hope precedes fear and boldness, for one first hopes for victory before he dares to confront evil (of which he treats in **q. 25**).

b. Specific Consideration

After the consideration of the passions in general, he treats of them specifically. And first those which pertain to the concupiscible, then those which pertain to the irascible.

1. Passions of the Concupiscible Appetite

The first passion of the concupiscible is love, of which there is a threefold treatment. First, the very notion of love is discussed; second, its cause; third, its effect. Concerning the nature and definition of love, he asks how love can be a passion, how it differs from intellectual love, which is *dilectio*, and how it differs from charity, which adds to ordinary love the esteem (*aestimatio*) of the beloved as something to be cherished, and finally how love is distinguished into the love of concupiscence and the love of friendship (**q. 26**)

Second, he treats the cause of love in **q. 27**, showing that love takes its origin from the good; the experience and knowledge of it; and the similitude it involves. He treats the effects of love in **q. 28**, that is, the things he takes to be caused by love, whether in the genus of formal, efficient, or final cause. In the genus of formal cause affective union with the beloved is the effect. Love causes many things in the genus of efficient cause, both in the apprehensive and in the appetitive parts. In the former it causes adhesion in the apprehensive part so that the lover adheres to and is occupied with thinking of the loved, and in the appetitive part, taking pleasure in the beloved which roots and anchors it in the heart. And if love is vehement it causes ecstasy insofar as one is borne outside himself in enjoying what is loved and does not merely remain within. This is truer of the love of friendship than the love of concupiscence, for concupiscence draws the thing to oneself rather than being borne toward it. Moreover, love causes zeal insofar as one is moved by love to sweep away every impediment to what is loved. Finally, it causes softness, removing the hardness of heart that impedes the loved thing from entering; enjoyment, when the loved thing is present, and languor or sadness, when it is absent; and fervor is caused by intense desire. Love causes all these things as an efficient cause. In the genus of final cause, it causes all the means which are desired because of the end loved.

The second passion of the concupiscible is desire, of which and its opposite he treats in **q. 30**.

The third passion of the concupiscible is pleasure or joy, whose opposite is sadness. He takes up four things with respect to delight. First, its nature (**q. 31**); second, the causes which generate delight, or by which we are disposed to it (**q. 32**); third, its effects, such that it dilates the heart causing thirst or desire and the like (**q. 33**); fourth, the moral goodness or badness of pleasure, and how it can be a measure of the moral insofar as it is the ultimate resting point (**q. 34**). Similarly, he treats of the opposite passion, which is sadness or sorrow. First, he considers its nature and its types (**q. 35**); second, the causes of sorrow (**q. 36**); third, its effects (**q. 37**); fourth, the remedies that can mitigate it (**q. 38**); fifth, the moral goodness or badness of sadness, for sadness can attach to a true or useful good, as we see in penance (**q. 39**).

2. Passions of the Irascible Appetite

First, Saint Thomas discusses hope, its nature, causes, and effects

Second, he treats despair in the same way, both hope and despair in **q. 40**.

Third, he considers fear in which, as with the other passions, he takes up four things. One, its nature and types (**q. 41**). Two, the object of fear, which is a future arduous evil. Guilt does not belong to fear as such, since guilt arises only with respect to will, and it is the effects of sin that must be especially feared. But the object of fear is the evil of pain and natural evil (**q. 42**). Three, he treats the cause of fear on the part of the one fearing (**q. 43**). Four, the effects of fear which imagination can bring about not only in appetite but also in the bodily powers by loss of spirit (**q. 44**).

Fourth, the passion in the irascible appetite which is called boldness or audacity, its nature, causes, and effect (**q. 45**).

Fifth, wrath, about which he considers three things. One, its nature and types, namely, madness and fury (**q. 46**). Two, the causes by which it originates or grows, especially from an injury or slight (**q. 47**). Three, the effects of wrath, for it causes a fervor of heart, disturbs the use of reason, and the like (**q. 48**).

Thus ends the treatise on human acts.

2. The Principles of Human Acts

As was said earlier, this treatise deals with the principles of human acts, and not just with any principles, but with efficient moral principles, whether intrinsic or extrinsic. The intrinsic are habits, virtuous or vicious, from which human acts proceed. The extrinsic principles are those which move us either by instruction, through law, or by aiding, as through grace.

a. Intrinsic Principles of Human Acts
1. Habits in General

In treating of habits Saint Thomas proceeds in his customary manner from the more to the less general. Thus he first treats habits in general, then virtuous habits in particular.

With respect to habits in general he does four things. First, he considers what habits are and the need to posit them (**q. 49**). Second, the subject to which they belong, both with respect to nature, which disposes us to them, and the powers, through which they act (**q. 50**). Third, he considers the causes of habits in three ways: one, with respect to their being and substance, insofar as they are acquirable by nature or are infused (**q. 51**); two, with respect to their increase, whether in intension or in extension (**q. 52**); three, with respect to their diminution or corruption (**q. 53**) Third, he considers their unity, plurality, and divisions, showing that in the same power there can be many habits although no habit is composed entitatively of several habits; as for their presently relevant division, he confines himself to good and bad (**q. 54**).

With respect to the specific treatment of habits, he does not discuss their atomic species, for those are treated in the Second Part of the Second Part, but rather their genera and general conditions and definitions of virtues and vices – of the virtues through q. 70, of vices and sins from qq. 71 through 89.

With regard to virtues, the two chief types of virtue are considered first, for some regulate human acts in the common and ordinary way, while others are from a higher prompting (*instinctum*) and regulation of the Holy Spirit: the first are called virtues, the second gifts.

2. Habits in Particular
a. On Virtues

With respect to the virtues, Saint Thomas considers five things. First, their essence; second, their subject; third, their distinction into different kinds; fourth, the causes of virtue; fifth, their general properties.

1. The Nature of Virtue

Saint Thomas explains the definition and nature of virtue by discussing its parts, namely, that it is a habit or quality, which is the genus, and that it is operative, which is the more common difference, and that it is morally good, which is the ultimate constitutive difference of virtue (**q. 55**).

2. The Subject of Virtue

As for the subject of virtue, Saint Thomas first removes from it what is not active and assigns as the subject of virtue only those powers of the soul which are capable of action but are undetermined. These are will, sense appetite, and intellect, with this difference that the virtues of will and appetite not only make the act good but the agent as well, because they rectify the inclination of the whole individual with respect to use and the task of execution. Intellectual virtues rectify operation in the attainment of truth as object, but they do not rectify the subject by inclining him with respect to perform-ance (q. 56).

3. Kinds of Virtue
a. Intellectual Virtues

As for the distinction or types of virtues, Saint Thomas first speaks of three kinds of virtue. Some are moral, some intel-lectual, and some theological. Man is either perfected in intel-lect in a natural way, something accomplished by intellectual virtue, or perfected morally with respect to will and appetite as ordered to the natural end, and this is accomplished by the acquired moral virtues, or he is perfected in a supernatural way, whether in intellect or will, and this by the theological virtues and other infused virtues which follow on them.

Saint Thomas treats the kinds of intellectual virtue in a single question. There are five kinds, three of which perfect the speculative part, namely the habit of the understanding of principles, wisdom, and science; two of which perfect the practical intellect, namely, prudence (which perfects in the order of things to be done, that is, directs the moral acts of man) and art (which perfects in the order of things to be made, that is, those works or effects which are made accord-ing to certain rules). These are the only habits that involve cer-titude and rectitude with respect to the true; other uncertain habits can permit a lapse into the false and thus do not per-fect the intellect with regard to its object which is the true: virtue is a disposition of the perfected (q. 57).

b. Moral Virtues

The second kind of virtues is the moral, and in explaining their distinct species he dwells on four things that can be con-sidered about them. (i) First, that from which they have their form and mode, namely, prudence. (ii) Second, that from which they have a matter to be moderated and ruled, name-ly, the passions or operations. (iii) Third, the species into which all the moral virtues are divided. (iv) Fourth, primary and secondary moral virtues. From all these can be gathered what pertains to the distinction and division of these virtues.

(i) With respect to the first of these, Saint Thomas shows that moral virtues are distinguished not only from the intellectual virtues of the speculative part, but also from those of the practical part, that is, from prudence. (*Pace* Socrates who spoke of all virtues as if there were prudence.) Nonetheless these virtues are ruled by prudence with respect to the determination of the means and the actual doing here and now. But prudence depends on the rectification of appetite with respect to the matter of the virtues as to the intention of the end; if one does not have the right intention he is not moved by it and cannot prudently judge. The rectification of intention with respect to the matter of the virtues pertains to the virtues themselves, not with respect to the ultimate and completive act, which is choice (moral virtues are elective habits), but with respect to the first and inchoative act by which appetite is disposed by virtue toward the end with respect to its matter. In this act it is not moved by prudence but by synderesis, which looks to the most universal principles and the common good. He shows the distinction of the virtues from prudence, yet their dependence on it, in **q. 58**.

(ii) The matter of the moral virtues is twofold: some virtues order the activities or movements of will, while others order the passions or movements of sense appetite. Passions are either inordinate and exceed the rule of reason, or they are ordered and subject to the rule of reason, or they are considered as susceptible of regulation. In the first sense, they are not the matter of virtue but are contrary to it. In the second sense they are acts elicited by virtue, for virtue is located in sense appetite in order to produce moderated or ruled passions. In the third sense they are the proper matter of the virtues because they are considered susceptible of the formal notion of virtue, which is regulation. However the virtues which look to the activities of will, such as justice, continence, and the like, do not have passions as the matter they must regulate, although they might have them as their effects, insofar as the motion of the higher part passes into the lower. So much for the comparison of virtues as to their matter and their distinction according to the different matters to be regulated (q. 59).

(iii) As for the third, he supposes that there is not just one virtue in will and appetite but several because the different matters regulable by different commands, though by one and the same ruling virtue, namely, prudence. They all proceed from its dictate or command because they are unified in one end of human life, but insofar as there are different matters to be regulated they receive regulation differently. Thus the distinction of moral virtue into its species is taken from the difference in proximate matter. For some, as we have said, moderate acts of will and others the passions of appetite. Some moderate acts of will and look to an operation that involves another in the light of what is owed in terms of equality – they belong to justice. But different virtues arise according to different notions of what is owed or of the equality to be achieved, and these are enumerated in the Second Part of the Second Part, q. 80. Others moderate acts of will with respect to the self, such as continence, humility, and the like. Virtues which concern the passions are diversified not only according to the diversity of the passions (since one virtue can moderate two opposed passions), but also according to degree of difficulty and the command (dictate) or regulating of the passion. Saint Thomas enumerates ten moral virtues dealing with the passions, namely, courage, temperance, liberality, magnificence, magnanimity, love of honor, gentleness, friendship, truth, diversion (*eutrapelia*). All these and others are treated in detail in the Second Part of the Second Part. For now he only indicates them generally (q. 60).

(iv) Fourth, he distinguishes principal and secondary moral virtues. Moral virtues can be considered primary either by comparison with the intellectual virtues, by a comparison of moral virtues among themselves or by comparison with different states, one of which is prior to another.

In the first way, moral virtues have primacy over the intellectual in their function and according to the definition of virtue because they rectify the very use and exercise of inclination by which a man is called good or bad absolutely. Intellectual virtues are primary by reason of operation and the attainment of their object, which they attain more abstractly and immaterially, for example, the true.

c. Cardinal Virtues

The second manner of comparison leads to the recognition of four cardinal or chief virtues in the moral order, namely, prudence, justice, fortitude, and temperance. They are said to be primary because they moderate prior and more difficult matters; those virtues are secondary or potential parts of the former because they moderate in the same way but in less difficult matters. The cardinal are also so called because the conditions required for virtue – discretion, rectitude, moderation, and firmness – are to be found especially in them.

The third way of ranking virtues is according to the different states in which the same virtues are found. This is the basis of distinguishing political virtues (which alone look to the common mode of acting in human society), the purifying virtues, those of the soul already purified, and the exemplar. This distinction is based on transcending human society and tending to assimilation with God, which with beginners are as purifying, in the perfected are of the purified soul, and in the divine state exemplars (all this in **q. 61**).

d. Theological Virtues

The theological virtues are the third kind of virtue. They are distinguished from the intellectual and moral because by them man is ordered to a higher end, namely, supernatural beatitude, which, since it exceeds our natural powers, requires that principles above nature be superadded to man that order him to such an end. These principles look to God himself, who is the supernatural end, and are therefore called theological virtues. They are three, because intellect and will must be perfected in order to tend toward the end. The intellect by supernatural revelation, thanks to which it knows the supernatural end, and this is faith, the first theological virtue. The will needs to be perfected in two ways, first with respect to the intention of the end, that it might pursue it: and since an end so beyond it relates to the will as arduous, will is first perfected by hope and then ordered to the end by perfect love, adhering to it and becoming one with it, and this charity does (q. 62).

4. The Causes of Virtue

Having explained the essence of the virtues, their subjects, division and varieties, he next turns to their causes and properties, and speaks first of the efficient cause of virtue in us, which is either by accustoming ourselves to their acts, when it is a question of acquired virtues, or infusion, in the case of the supernatural virtues (q. 63).

5. The Properties of Virtue

Finally he takes up the properties of the virtues, which are four. First, to hold to the mean, avoiding by regulation excess and defect in the matter regulated. Second, that there be a connection between them and the rational principle from which all regulation comes, that is, to prudence. Third, their inequality, due to the fact that the regulable matter participates in the order of reason differently. Fourth, permanence, whether in this life or beyond it as well (though in another state) because of the permanence of the subject (q. 64).

With respect to the first property, namely, the mean of virtue: this belongs to all the moral virtues because their matter can be moderated and can by excess or defect depart from the mean of reason. It does not belong to the theological virtues which look to God himself for their matter and not that which may or may not be ruled by him (q. 65).

As for the second property, the connection of the virtues, this does not belong to them by reason of the matter which they govern (which are the different passions which are not connected among themselves) nor by reason of their specifying form (that is, the different formal objects of the virtues), but by reason of the ordering and directing form, which is prudence and requires the rectification of intention in the matter of all the virtues in order that it might direct them to choose rightly. The virtues are also unified in a higher form ordering them to the supernatural end, that is, in charity, for which all the virtues are required since charity fulfills the whole law. But in an imperfect state virtues can remain unconnected among themselves.

The third property, the inequality of the virtues – whether by comparing the intellectual with the moral, or the theological with both, or the moral among themselves where inequality can obtain even though they are regulated by the same principle, prudence, still in themselves they receive a different regulation and thus different formal notions according to the good of reason because of their different matter (**q. 66**).

Concerning the fourth property, he shows which virtues endure after this life and which do not. Some simply pass away, such as faith and hope, because of the loss of their objects, which is the unseen and not-had. So too virtues of sense appetite because of a defect in the subject do not remain in the separated soul. But other virtues change their mode and state because of the different way in which the separated soul operates (**q. 67**).

b. On the Gifts

Up to this point Saint Thomas has treated virtues properly so called. There remains to consider those which surpass the usual regulation of virtues because they proceed from a higher measure. They are not immediately measured by the rules of reason and its ordinary mode of operating but by the rule and movement of the Holy Spirit. That is why they are called gifts: their measure transcends the mode due to humans as such. He takes up three things: the nature of such gifts, how they are distinguished from virtues, and their number. Then he turns to the two kinds of act which follow from them, namely, the beatitudes and the fruits of the Holy Spirit.

1. How Gifts Differ from Virtues

With respect to the first point, Saint Thomas notes that properly speaking, virtue, since it is the perfect disposition of a power and the utmost of which it is capable, perfects the power in the same order as the power. The utmost in anything is of the same nature as that of which it is the utmost so that if a power is raised above its mode and order, this is by something more than virtue and is a special Gift of the Holy Spirit. In this sense, all supernatural habits can be called Gifts of the Holy Spirit, but they differ because some supernatural habits, although in substance – that is, with respect to the object and the end which specifies them – they are supernatural, but are measured by the mode of reason, that is, what reason can attain when given a supernatural light. But there are some habits which incline us to follow the movement of the Holy Spirit, not within the ordinary rules of reason and its limited modes, but by a measure proper to him. Such habits exceed in substance and mode the notion of virtue and in a special way are called gifts – Isaiah ix, 2, calls them spirits – since the mind is moved not by human exertion or in the human manner, but from the movement and breathing of the Holy Spirit ruling in a special way. Thus the different movement, ruling as well as effective, distinguishes the Gifts of the Holy Spirit from the virtues which can also be called gifts because of infusion. They presuppose a man conjoined to the Holy Spirit by grace and the theological virtues that he might be easily moved by him. The Holy Spirit moves the intellect and will in a more universal way; the intellect by four gifts, which elevate the mind that it might know of God and counsel about things to be done. The gift of understanding penetrates the things revealed by God; the gift of knowledge judges them from effects taken to be the effects of God; the gift of wisdom judges divine things from the taste and experience of them; the gift of counsel discerns what is to be done. Three gifts are perfective of will. With respect to everything that concerns others, a man is moved by the gift of piety, insofar as through grace he considers God as Father and other men as brothers; with respect to what pertains to the concupiscible, a man is perfected by the gift of fear, which draws one back from evil desires; with respect to what pertains to the irascible, he is perfected by the gift of courage (q. 68).

2. The Beatitudes

Both the beatitudes and the Fruits are acts that follow on the gifts, but the beatitudes are the most excellent because by a special movement of the Holy Spirit they bring man close to and assimilate him to the fulfilling beatitude which is in the fatherland, thanks to which proximity and hope they are called beatitudes and were given as eight by Christ Our Lord (Matthew 5, 3–11). Poverty of spirit, which empties the heart of every creature, is a most excellent act proceeding from the Holy Spirit. And so with the rest (**q. 69**).

3. The Fruits

Fruits too are called acts of the gifts. However, they are not as special and excellent as the beatitudes, but more common and ordinary. Twelve are enumerated by the Apostle Paul in Galatians 5, 22: "The fruit of the Holy Spirit is charity, joy," etc. They are treated in **q. 70**.

c. On Vices and Sins

Following the treatise on the virtues there remains to consider vice and sin, something Saint Thomas does in **qq. 71–89**. First he considers sin absolutely in its essence; then he considers it according to what belongs to it in comparison with and relation to its object, subject, causes, and effects.

1. The Nature of Sin

What pertains to the essence of sin, whether it is an act or a habit, and how it is contrary to virtue and the root of virtue, namely, rational nature, is discussed in **q. 71**.

Sin can be considered, first, with regard to its objects and circumstances and the other principles by which sins are distinguished. Second, sins are compared in terms of gravity, likeness, inequality, and so forth. Third, he considers the subject capable of sin. Fourth, the causes of sin. Fifth, the effects of sin.

The first is treated in **q. 72**, where he discusses all the principles which can distinguish sins, speaking generally; for example, object, circumstances, effects, consequent condemnation, causes, and other like things.

The second, namely the gravity and inequality of sins, and the causes aggravating sin, are dealt with in **q. 73**.

The third, namely, the subject of sin, is discussed in **q. 74**. Not indeed the subject *which*, or the individual, but the subject *in which*, or the powers capable of sin. By way of participation sin is in other powers which have some share in freedom.

Fourth, sin is related to quasi-efficient or disposing causes (the material cause pertains to the subject; the final to the end, of which he has already spoken; the formal to specification, of which he will speak when he considers the species of sin individually in the Second Part of the Second Part). He first treats the cause of sin in general, then in particular.

2. The Causes of Sin

In general, he distinguishes the interior and exterior cause of sin.

As for the interior cause, either it refers to specification on the part of the object or to the subject with respect to execution. The apparent good, in disharmony with reason, is a cause on the side of the object, but because the good does not move unless it is proposed, there is added on the side of the object the reason which defectively proposes it, because it ought to regulate that act and does not. As for disposing causes, there are the internal and external senses and sense appetite, because as a person is, so does the end appear to him, and the object appears differently because of different dispositions of appetite and passion. On the part of the subject there is the will as free, which is a power that inclines the whole subject.

As for the exterior causes, these can be efficient, disposing, or final. Anyone showing or proposing an object can be an external efficient cause, but only as proposing; only God can move as an efficient cause within the will. As for disposing or final cause, one sin can be the cause of another, either because one act disposes for another like it, as gluttony disposes for lust, and avarice to litigation. Or one can be the final cause of another, as one who steals in order to commit fornication. It is for this reason that from the capital sins which deal with most desirable things other sins arise. He treats of causes of sin in general in **q. 75**.

In particular. First he treats internal then external causes. There are three internal causes, namely the reason proposing, the sensitive appetite enticing and disposing for the proposal of the object, and the basely disposed will. On the side of reason, it is clear that [right] reason itself plays no role in sin, but its opposite, practical ignorance, and the defect in right regulation or lack of consideration, do. He discusses such ignorance in **q. 76**. On the part of sense appetite, passion moves the will, as it were, incidentally and mediately, either by distracting reason or also by impeding it if it is strong, or by enticement, making the object appear fitting by stirring up images. He treats of the way in which passion is a cause of sin, and how it might alleviate or excuse sin, how it can lead to deliberate consent, and other like things in **q. 77**.

On the part of the will, malice, which is an inordinate and depraved disposition of will and comes about because of attachment to the temporal good and not caring about any spiritual damage, causes sin. It makes the intellect judge practically in such a way that between two goods, the one spiritual and better, the other temporal and lesser, it is willing to suffer the loss of the better good, knowing it to be better, rather than dismiss the lesser because of the will's adhesion to the latter. Thus by certain choice one is said to sin, that is, to choose the defective as something less than God and, as it were, deliberately because of an evil disposition and the perverse condition of the will. One who sins from habit, sins from certain malice (**q. 78**).

As for the external causes of sin, they are either God as efficient cause, or, by way of suggestion or persuasion, the devil and man. God does not cause the sin but is efficient cause merely of that to which the sin attaches, of whatever in it is positive or perfect and proceeding from the power of nature as well as from the author of nature. He is not cause of the defect or imperfection and the turning from God and rationality. From him comes nothing positive as to the defect which is reduced to a deficient principle and is from nothing (**q. 79**)

The devil is the cause of sin by tempting and suggesting,

that is, moving by way of proposing the object or altering images and imaginative species (**q. 80**).

As for man, [Saint Thomas] distinguishes various ways in which man is the cause of sin. One man can cause another's sin by suggesting and proposing an object. There is no special difficulty with this: he acts in the same way the devil does though not so subtly. Another way man causes another's sin is by way of generation, namely, original sin by which other sins are in a way caused. There are three things to take into account here. First, its transmission, namely, how it can be passed from one to another. Second, its essence. Third, its subject. He shows transmission to be possible because, although sin is a voluntary defect, if there is a sin of nature, it suffices that it be voluntary by the will of the nature or principle propagating the nature. For the will of nature is the will of the head of the entire nature whose voluntarily elicited action has a voluntary effect in every nature derived from and propagated by him, since these are, as it were, his members. Thus the sin transmitted is not actual sin or by way of an act, that could not be transmitted to the child since he does nothing; rather it is a sin in the manner of an effect transmitted from the first head and is called voluntary, not as elicited but as terminating, because it is a certain term, that is, privation or stain derived by the act of the sinner's will which in the first man was virtually present along with all the other voluntary acts of his progeny (**q. 81**).

The nature of this sin can be put together from the foregoing: it is not actual sin, but habitual, that is, a stain of sin habitually and permanently left by sin – this expresses both what is formal and what is material in this sin. What is *formal* in this stain is the privation of the glory of grace and the splendor of reason; it is not a pure physical privation (for then it would rather have the note of punishment) but a moral or voluntary privation which derives from its relation to the will of the one who caused it, that is, the will of our first parent as head of all, who might have communicated grace to all if he had not sinned, but transmitted its privation by sinning. And just as every other sin consists of a stain due to a voluntary privation, so it is with the original stain, though in the other sins only the person who sins is stained. What is *material* in this sin is called concupiscence, that is, the infection and dissolution of all the powers of the soul. Not that this is a matter constituting the sin as if it were a part or element, but it is a matter corrupted and infected by this sin as its effect, insofar as it not only removes grace but also the gift of original justice by which the powers of the soul were under the subject's control. This is similar to saying that the heart or head or entrails are the matter of an illness, because the illness corrupts them. Thus unrestrained and infected concupiscence is the material of original sin as an effect subsequent to it, as the organic body is the matter of the soul and caused by it (**q. 82**).

With respect to the subject of original sin, he shows it to be the soul and not the flesh, because the flesh is not capable of sin in the way of a subject, although it is the instrument of transmitting this sin by means of generating. It is the cause of transmission because it is the means of generating the whole man, soul and flesh. When the soul of the infant is joined to the flesh prepared by the act of generation, the infant is joined by way of consequence to the first parent and head of whom this child is a member detached from him. Because the stain of sin is immediately in the essence of the soul, which is the subject of grace and hence too of its privation; it was also the subject of original justice, so the stain of original sin is directly in the essence of the soul. Thus it disorders the powers of the soul radically and infects both the rational and the sensitive powers capable of sin, but the generative power only as an instrument of human propagation (**q. 83**).

Finally, after the quasi-efficient external and internal causes of sin, he treats the disposing or final cause, insofar as one sin is the cause of another. This can be either in the form of demerit, insofar as God, because of one sin permits man to fall into another (something not treated here), or as the disposing or final cause of another sin. Generally speaking, there are two principles of sin, cupidity and pride, the former as providing a matter for all the sins, the latter as seeking one's own excellence and perfection. More particularly however the sins that are more desirable also have the note of end, insofar as from them others originate and are done as means for the sake of them. These are called capital sins because the end is the head and principle of those which are ordered to the end (q. 84).

3. The Effects of Sin

There are three effects of sin, speaking generally. First, with respect to the good of nature. Second, with respect to the stain on the soul. Third, with respect to the punishment of guilt.

As for the good of nature, sin removes some things completely, only diminishes others, and yet others it neither removes nor diminishes. It removes totally grace and the gift of original justice which was a good conferred on the whole nature. On this follow other bodily effects, such as death and the things that lead to death, such as illness, infirmity, and so on. It diminishes the inclination or relation to the good, not indeed by erasing it, since its root which is nature, remains, but by bringing out impediments and sluggishness (*retardationem*) to reaching the good appropriate to the nature. It neither removes nor diminishes nature itself and its properties (q. 85).

The stain on the soul, by which the soul is deprived of the refulgence of the natural light and of the light of grace, is the second effect of original sin, as a shadow is to body, blocking the source of light. Insofar as a cause is a greater or lesser impediment, the privation is greater or lesser, and the more impediments the greater the privation. So it is with stain and the multiplication of sins (q. 86).

As for the punishment of guilt, original sin binds the sinner to this. In some sins it is a question of temporal punishment, as in venial sins; in others, the mortal, it takes away orientation to the ultimate end, which of itself is irreparable by a movement of conversion and thus entails an eternal punishment. Of this, and the way in which one sin is punishment for another, he treats in q. 87.

Because venial and mortal sins are distinguished by the different punishments they entail, he discusses their distinction with reference to two things. First, by a comparison of one to the other, how they are distinct, and how one can come about without the other (q. 88). Second, he treats especially of venial sin and the stain it causes in the soul not by depriving it of grace but of fervor or by retarding the extension of grace to things which can be done with its help. He also discusses the subjects in which it can and cannot be. All this in **q. 89.**

b. Extrinsic Principles of Human Acts

Having explained the intrinsic principles of human acts, which are virtuous and vicious habits, Saint Thomas goes on to discuss the extrinsic principles of human acts. They are called extrinsic not because they do not posit something intrinsic in the soul – grace of course does –, but because what is imprinted on the soul is not an interior principle of motion, but is imprinted by an exterior cause in order that man might be moved. It is common to every mover that it impress something intrinsic on what it moves, and the subject impressed operates as subordinate to the external mover. Thus absolutely speaking it is called an extrinsic principle. Saint Thomas calls habits intrinsic causes of human acts because they are the fulfillment of a power and thus are subordinate to the soul itself as moving principle. If they are supernatural, however, they come about and are impressed by an extrinsic principle and are discussed under the heading of grace, as being habitual grace.

Setting aside then the extrinsic principle which can move to good or evil by way of persuasion or suggestion, which has already been treated, Saint Thomas here treats of the extrinsic principle which moves to the good universally, something that comes about in two ways, either by instructing and regulation, which law does, or by helping and moving, which grace does. He discusses law from qq. 90–108, and grace from qq. 109–114.

1. Laws

In his customary manner, Saint Thomas begins with a general consideration of law and then goes on to specifics.

In the general consideration, he takes up three things: its essence, its kinds, and its more common effects. He considers its essence in **q. 90**, showing that law is an ordinance fashioned by the one ruling a multitude. Because it is an ordinance it pertains formally to intellect which compares and orders things; because it is efficacious, it presupposes will; and because it relates to many, it requires promulgation. The division of law into various kinds, eternal, natural, human, and so forth, is done in **q. 91**. The more common effects intended by law are three, namely, to prohibit evils, to command goods, and to permit things which are neither (**q. 92**).

In particular, Saint Thomas teaches that there are six kinds of law: the eternal law (**q. 93**), which is in the mind of God governing all things; natural law, which is naturally impressed on us, and enlightens the principles of the practical order; human law, which is derived from natural law by legitimate authority; divine positive law, which is twofold, the Old and the New; finally, the law of the flesh, which comes from the corruption of original sin (he has already discussed this in discussing original sin). He treats natural law in **q. 94**, and then human law in three questions. First, he treats its nature and origin in natural law, the conditions required for it to be correct, and its subdivision (**q. 95**). Then he considers its force and execution, for example, to what matters and persons it applies and what obligation it imposes (**q. 96**). Finally, he takes up the mutability of human law, whether absolutely, when it is abrogated, or partially, when it is dispensed (**q. 97**).

As for divine positive law, he first treats of the Old Law, then the New Law. With respect to the Old Law, he first considers it in general; then, its precepts. The general consideration deals with its conditions – how it was given, when, and how it obliges (**q. 98**). As for its precepts, he first considers them in general, showing that it contained three types of precept. First, the moral principles which dispose human acts generally; second, the ceremonial, which pertain to the worship of God by that people; third, the judicial precepts, pertaining to the rule of the people (**q. 99**). Then he treats of each type.

Moral precepts. These are contained in the Decalogue; what they are, their obligatoriness, their dispensability, and whether they prescribe both the substance and mode of virtue (**q. 100**).

Ceremonial precepts. He takes up three things. First, the division of ceremonial precepts, of which there are four kinds – some concern sacrifice; some deal with the sacred, that is, as instruments serving divine worship; some concern the sacraments and legal sanctifications; some are observances in food and drink, and so forth (**q. 101**). Second, he considers the literal and figurative causes of these precepts, because they prefigure and announce the coming of Christ and his redeeming acts, and thus are made obsolete when Christ consummates redemption on the cross: they are then a dead law with respect to their meaning, though their observance fades away little by little in order that they might be buried with honor (**q. 103**).

Judicial precepts. Two questions are devoted to these. He first treats of them as such, showing that what the law determined with respect to judgments did not directly prefigure or announce Christ as the ceremonial do. Hence there is no sin involved if they be observed in a republic, though they do not now oblige since the whole law was ceased (**q. 104**). Second, he divides judicial precepts into four kinds. For some order the rule and judgment of princes, others of citizens, others relations with aliens, yet others deal with domestic rule (**q. 105**).

After the Old Law, he takes up the New and briefly discusses three things. First, this law in itself, its power to justify and its duration until the end of the world (**q. 106**). Second, he compares the New Law to the Old, showing how the latter fulfills the former, and that it is not more onerous thanks to charity and freedom, although it is more difficult because of the greater perfection it involves (**q. 107**). Third, he considers the matter of evangelical law, both with respect to interior and external acts, and with respect to precepts and counsels (**q. 108**).

2. Grace
a. The Nature of Grace

The consideration of grace follows that of law and involves a treatise with three parts. Saint Thomas first considers grace itself; second its cause; third its effect.

As for grace itself, he considers three things in three questions. First, its necessity, which pertains to the question *an est* (whether it is), and its kinds. For by the term grace we understand generally speaking something given gratuitously and not owed to the receiver. Since in acting the creature depends on God in two ways, in the form or power which is the reason for acting, and in the application by which it is moved to act, to both of these God can add a gratuitous good, namely the form or power of acting, whether proximate – charity – or radical – grace. He can also add a gratuitous aid to the motion or application to act. Saint Thomas shows the necessity of grace with respect to both of these, on the part of intellect in order to know the truth, and on the part of the will in order to attain the good. What grace is and that it is needed in the state of corrupt nature in order to effect perfect works of the healthy man, that he might fulfill the whole law, love God above all things, rise from sin, persevere in the good and avoid sins; and also how it is required in the state of integral nature especially for supernatural works – all these he takes up in **q. 109.**

Second, as to the essence of grace, he shows it to be a habitual quality; shows how it differs from operative qualities, and that sanctifying grace resides in the essence of the soul (**q. 110**).

Third, Saint Thomas discusses the division of grace into operative and cooperative, prevenient and subsequent, *gratum facientem* and *gratis datam* (**q. 111**). He does not express here its sufficiency and efficacy, but in discussing it as an aid, he discusses its power or form, which is sufficient, and its applying motion, which is efficacious.

b. The Causes of Grace

There is a threefold cause of grace: efficient, disposing, and instrumental. He will treat of it as instrument in the Third Part when he takes up the sacraments. Here he discusses its effectiveness and disposing causes. The principle efficient cause of grace is God alone; the disposing, the act of free will, insofar as it is moved to God by a supernatural aid (**q. 112**).

c. The Effects of Grace

He considers two effects of grace, the formal effect of sanctifying grace which is justification; that and its causes, and the order and manner of their coming about, he discusses in **q. 113**. Another effect proceeds from sanctifying and cooperating grace, and this is merit, both of eternal life as well as increase of grace. For the first grace and the last, namely, perseverance, since they depend solely on the actual help and motion which is the principle of all grace, do not fall under merit. He discusses this effect in **q. 114**.

Detailed Outline of
The Second Part of the Second Part

The Second Part of the Second Part

The Order and Connections of Its Treatises

Particular Human Acts

[1. Man's Ultimate End]
[2. Properly Human Acts]
[a. In General]

b. In Particular
After the general consideration of human acts, in the Second
Part of the Second Part Saint Thomas treats them in particular, that is, according to the specific definitions of virtues and
vices.

In order that moral matters might be treated in their totality, Saint Thomas, proceeding from the more to the less common, distinguishing those which pertain to all men and concern the common state from those which pertain to special
states of life.

1. Virtues and Vices of the Common State of Life
There are virtues and vices relevant to the common state of
men, to which all are inclined by reason and will. Virtues are
either intellectual, theological, or moral. He does not treat of
the intellectual virtues here because they are not directly relevant to human acts as moral, although as Gifts of the Holy
Spirit, namely, knowledge, wisdom, and understanding, he
will discuss them in this treatise because they correspond to

the theological virtues. The proper task at present is to treat the theological and moral virtues. There are three theological virtues – faith, hope, and charity. The chief moral virtues are the cardinal virtues to which other less important virtues are reduced. The cardinal virtues are prudence, justice, fortitude, and temperance. Saint Thomas treats each of them as follows: first the virtue itself; second the opposed vice; third the Gift of the Holy Spirit corresponding to it; fourth, the precept, if there be one, of that virtue. This treatment continues through **q. 170**.

The virtues pertaining to special states of life are treated from **q. 171** to the end of the part, not dealing with those proper to political or civil life but only those that relate to theological or ecclesiastical states – as we noted above when we gave a general overview of the Second Part of the Second Part, and will speak of more fully below treating each of these states in particular. This then is the first division of this part, into a treatment of what pertains to the common moral life of men; the second, a treatment of what pertains to special states.

a. The Theological Virtues
1. Faith

Saint Thomas begins the special treatment of virtues with the first theological virtue, faith, and divides the treatise, in the order mentioned, into four parts. First, he treats the virtue itself; secondly the Gifts of the Holy Spirit corresponding to it; third, the opposed vices; fourth, the precepts which have been given concerning faith: **qq. 1–16**.

a. Faith Itself

As for the virtue of faith itself, three things are discussed: First, the object which specifies it; second, its acts, both interior and external, which are more immediately specified by the object; third, faith as a habit through which the act is specified.

1. The Object of Faith

First, he discusses the formal notion of the object of faith and two conditions demanded by that object. The formal notion is the First Truth Revealing. The conditions are two. First, that what is thus revealed (since it is revealed by the intermediary of divine testimony) is not seen or known with evidence but is obscure. The second condition is that it be proposed through an infallible instrument or organ, which for us is the Church or its supreme head, the Roman Pontiff. For the first founders of the faith who have passed it on to us, there was an immediate revelation from God or a revelation by the ministry of an angel. Of the specification and conditions of faith he treats in **q. 1**.

2. The Act of Faith

Of its act, which is immediately specified by its object, he next treats. On the interior act of faith and of its necessity and of the things which a man is held explicitly to believe, he treats in **q. 2**. The exterior act, which is the confession of faith, and its necessity for salvation, is treated in **q. 3**.

3. The Habit of Faith

After the act of faith, he takes up the habit of faith, which is specified by means of the act. There are four things to take into account. First, the habit itself; second, its material cause, which is the subject; third, its efficient cause; fourth, its effect on the soul. The first is considered in **q. 4**, namely, how the habit of faith is a virtue, how unformed faith differs from formed faith, and how it relates to the other virtues. The second is considered in **q. 5**, namely, its subject, both the subject in which (*quo*), as well as the subject which (*quod*), that is, the angels while they are on the way (*viatores*) and men who are not infidels, but not the damned or heretics. He treats the third in **q. 6**, showing how even unformed faith is infused by God. The fourth he takes up in **q. 7**, showing that besides the acts of faith which are elicited by it, two other acts are attributed to it as moving and directing, namely, fear, because of God's supreme excellence which he reveals to us, and purity of heart, which is the beginning of justification in the will and expels errors from intellect.

b. Gifts Corresponding to Faith

Having explained the virtue of faith with respect to act and habit, he goes on to discuss the second item, namely, the Gifts of the Holy Spirit corresponding to it, which are two, the gift of understanding and the gift of knowledge. Since assenting to what is to be believed is the chief act of faith, and these exceed the natural light, being supernatural things, man must be given a light to penetrate and grasp them, as well as the strength or ability to judge and discern them: no one can give a firm and certain assent, which is the ultimate resolution of intellect, who does not first penetrate and grasp or apprehend well that to which he assents, and at the same time discern and judge what things must be, and what things must not be, assented to. In order to assent to the truth of a thing for its own sake one must first understand and grasp and apprehend that truth in itself, that is, grasp the revelation of the thing itself revealed. In faith, which is a revelation testifying obscurely, the intellect must grasp the thing as testified or credible. In a clear revelation, such as occurs in the Fatherland, outside the Word and outside the light of glory, it must grasp and understand the revelation. In this life, the gift of understanding differs from faith because faith is ordered to assenting to what is to be believed because of the authority of the speaker, whereas the gift of understanding penetrates and grasps the credibility itself, or the testimony. But in the Fatherland it is ordered to grasping and penetrating those clear revelations outside the Word, not to assenting to revealed things. Such penetration and understanding is a Gift of the Holy Spirit when one understands by union or connaturality with the very things revealed or with the revelation itself, as had by the movement of the Holy Spirit (1 John 2, 27): "His anointing teaches you concerning all things." The statement is a formal one: insofar as he anoints, he teaches; oil both lights and anoints, but the Gift of the Holy Spirit teaches, not insofar as it illumines, but insofar as it anoints, that is, insofar as it affects and connaturalizes or accustoms us to supernatural things. Thus it is distinguished from the light of glory in the Father land because the light of glory by the very effectiveness of light penetrates to the divine essence; Psalm

35, 10: "In your light we see light." But the gift of understanding, by anointing and connaturalizing to supernatural
things, penetrates them (**q. 8**).

He treats the gift of knowledge in **q. 9**. This is distinguished from the gift of understanding, the gift of wisdom
and from faith itself, because knowledge judges something by
way of its causes. Faith does not judge discursively the things
proposed for belief, or their truth or credibility, but assents
out of obedience to the testimony of God. Similarly the gift of
understanding does not make a judgment by discussing a
thing in its causes but only penetrates and grasps the thing
itself. Therefore the gift of knowledge is distinguished from
both because it judges of things to be believed according to
some cause or merit of credibility, and this pertains to the
judgment of discretion or discussion. It differs from the gift of
wisdom because of the means or cause through which it
judges, for it pertains to wisdom to judge through the
supreme and highest cause, but knowledge judges through a
lesser cause. If then one judges and discerns the things to be
believed out of some union or connaturality with God, insofar as one tastes of his goodness, that is the gift of wisdom,
and it corresponds with charity, which unites us to God by
love and taste. If he judges of things to be believed by way of
a kind of union with God as revealing in time, he discerns
what has been revealed from what has not, and what is to be
believed from what is not. He is said to have knowledge
because he judges according to some temporal effect, not simply according to affectivity.

c. Vices Opposed to Faith

The third topic has to do with the vices opposed to faith.
Three vices can be opposed to it, either directly to faith itself
and its interior act, to its external act, namely, confessing the
faith, or to the gifts corresponding to faith.

1. Infidelity

Infidelity is opposed to faith itself, not purely negatively, as
would be the case with someone who had heard nothing of
the faith, for that is rather a pain that a fault, but privative

infidelity, which does not acquiesce in the faith known. There are three kinds of infidelity: paganism, Judaism, and heresy, which cover many errors insofar as different things are denied. He treats of infidelity and the things connected to it in **q. 10**. Because of their peculiar difficulties, he treats specially of heresy and apostasy: of heresy in **q. 11**, and of apostasy in **q. 12**.

2. Blasphemy

Blasphemy is opposed to confessing the faith: it is the derogation of some excellent goodness, particularly the divine. There are two things to consider about this sin. First, in itself and in general, in **q. 13**. Second, in particular the blasphemy which is the sin against the Holy Spirit, when a man directly poses an obstacle to the remission of sins, or removes the things whereby the Holy Spirit impedes our choice of sin. Because the remission of sins is appropriated to the Holy Spirit these are called sins against the Holy Spirit. There are six, namely, despair, presumption, impenitence, obstinacy of heart, impugning the known truth, and envy of fraternal grace. Of these only final impenitence is absolutely unforgivable, both in this world and in the next; the others are called irremissible because of the special difficulty they pose for remission, insofar as such sins of their very kinds create an impediment and reject the remedy of sins: in some such way illnesses are called incurable. The infinite power of the Holy Spirit can conquer such resistance (**q. 14**).

3. Sins Opposed to Faith

Three sins are opposed to the gifts corresponding to faith. Ignorance is opposed to knowledge: how it is a sin was treated in IaIIae, q. 76. Blindness and dullness of mind are opposed to the gift of understanding, for they are the privation of spiritual light. This privation is sometimes said to be only the penalty for sin: Wisdom 2, 21: "Malice has blinded them." Here malice is given as the cause of blindness, but sometimes there is a voluntary loss of the intellectual light, as we read in Psalm 35, 4: "They did not wish to understand how they might act well." Or out of excess desire for temporal things one is dulled and does not understand: "Fire fell upon them" (that is, inordinate concupiscence) "and they did not see the sun," that is, spiritual light. He treats these sins in **q. 15**.

Finally he treats of the precepts stating what is to be believed by faith, and the acts of the gifts of knowledge and understanding, in **q. 16**.

2. Hope

Saint Thomas follows the same order in discussing hope as he did in discussing faith, considering four things: first, hope itself; second, the gift corresponding to it; three, the opposite vices; four, precepts concerning the act of hope.

a. Hope Itself

As for hope itself, there are two things to take up: the definition or essence of the virtue of hope, and its subject. Whatever is formal should be considered in defining hope: first, the notion of its specifying object, which is the good to be enjoyed, that is, God, as something difficult, taking 'difficult' not only passively, as something far exceeding our capacity, but also actively, as that which overcomes the difficulty, which is the assistance of God. The second formality is the definition of virtue, and then of a kind of virtue, namely, the theological, that is, a virtue having God for its object or matter to be attained; then its difference from other virtues; and finally its relation to faith and charity (**q. 17**).

As for the subject of hope, he discusses both the subject in which (*quo*), the will as being in an eminent manner irascible and thus confronting the difficult, and the subject which (*quod*), the person who hopes and may be anyone in this state of life. Hope is certain thanks to divine assistance but contingent from the point of view of the subject's relation to a future event. Hope is found neither in the blessed nor in the damned (**q. 18**).

b. Corresponding Gift

Second, as to the Gift of the Holy Spirit corresponding to

hope, namely, the gift of fear. This is a filial fear, Saint Thomas explains, and is to be distinguished from mundane or servile fear, which is contrary to it, since mundane fear is evil, fearing to lose worldly things even when they are against God, but Thomas chooses to proceed from the imperfect to the perfect. Servile fear fears to lose God because of punishment, but filial fear because of himself and because of guilt. There are different levels of filial fear. Initially it is imperfect, as in beginners, who fear rather the evil that is guilt but still retain some fear of the evil of punishment. Perfect filial fear does not so much fear evil itself directly, whether of guilt or punishment, but God himself whom it reveres as omnipotent, not only as able to do good but also as able to inflict at least the evil of annihilation and destruction. Thus it brings about a contractive movement in the soul which reflects on one's own littleness. It looks to the divine good, not as pursuable, but as something that might be spurned, with the implication of possible evil (**q. 19**).

c. Opposed Vices

Third, there are two vices opposed to hope, namely, despair and presumption. Despair, because it destroys the note of something future or possible and thus one despairs of attaining it. Presumption destroys the note of the difficult, thinking it easy to achieve such a good, for example, without merits or without the required help. He discusses despair in **q. 20** and presumption in **q. 21**.

d. The Precepts of Hope

Finally, he treats the precepts of hope, and the fear corresponding to it, in **q. 22**.

3. Charity

Four principal things are taken up with regard to this virtue, though sometimes Saint Thomas's accustomed order is altered because of the demands of doctrine. He treats charity and the vices opposed to it before taking up the gift corresponding to it because many virtues and their effects arise from charity, for which reason there are many opposed vices.

That is why he first treats these vices and virtues before the gift. Here then is the order of treatment: First, he discusses charity in itself; second, its acts and effects, or the virtues stemming from it; third, vices opposed both to charity and these virtues; fourth, the precepts of charity; fifth, the gift corresponding to it; sixth, the sins opposed to this gift.

a. The Virtue of Charity

Charity is first considered in itself, both absolutely, insofar as it is the virtue of supernatural friendship with God, and of the love which attains him in himself and for himself immediately: here Saint Thomas explains its formal object, namely, the goodness of God in itself as this is communicable through friendship. It is because it maximally attains the end of all the other virtues that charity is the greatest of them all, moving the others (**q. 23**). He also considers it comparatively, in relation to the subject in which charity exists and as ordered to the material object with which it is concerned.

As for the subject, he considers that in which charity resides, namely, the will, and the conditions it takes on in this subject. The first of these conditions is that it is infused by God alone since only God can enter into the will. The second, that it is increased in the subject insofar as it is present in it with greater or lesser intensity, although it has no term of increase on the side of the principle infusing it. The third, that it has different states in the subject: the charity of beginners, of the proficient, and of the perfect. Four, that it can be acquired and lost by mutable will (**q. 24**).

As for the material object of charity, Saint Thomas takes up two things. First, what are its objects. Second, the order in which charity looks to those objects. The objects to which charity extends are taken from the formal reason of their tending to God, namely, a friendship that is based on a communication of divine and supernatural goods. It must therefore look first to God as the author of such goods. Secondarily, it bears on everything that can share in such supernatural goods with us, and these are: angels, and men, even sinners who can yet be converted, and even our bodies which are instruments serving virtue, but not the demons or the damned since they are incapable of supernatural goods. He treats of these objects in **q. 25**. The principles of the order to be observed among the objects of charity, namely, that God is to be loved primarily, and that those neighbors of greater and more excellent goodness and those most closely related to one are to be most loved, are discussed in **q. 26**.

b. The Acts and Effects of Charity

We distinguish the acts of charity from its effects, because the act of charity is properly elicited by this virtue whereas the effect is what is commanded, results impressed by or left by such a virtue, whether in the way of redundancy or command.[1] Accordingly, Saint Thomas treats first the act and then the effects of charity.

The act is love, which he not only calls simple benevolence, but also adds the note of affective union with the other. He shows how charity relates to God, to friends, and to enemies, and how this love is more or less meritorious toward friend or enemy (**q. 27**).

The interior effects of charity – Insofar as all virtues are commanded by charity, they are affected by it as being directed to the end of charity: that is why charity is called the form of the virtues. Here he does not treat this effect, but rather special effects which arise from the act of love, for we say that the act of love implies benevolence with some kind of affective union with what is loved. From the note of affective union arise two interior effects of charity, namely, joy and peace. These do not require a virtue distinct from charity since they do not add any special formal note to it or address any difficulty in the object of charity: joy is an act, or passion, caused by the union with the beloved as interiorly present (**q. 28**). As for peace, it is tranquility of order, and concord or harmony is the ordered union of hearts pertaining to the state or disposition left by charity according to the affectionate union with friends (**q. 29**).

---

1   See Cardinal Cajetan's commentary on IIaIIae, q. 36, a. 3, ad 2; q. 39, a. 1, ad 2, dubium; q. 81, a. 1, 4 and 5; and especially q. 144, a. 1, ad 5.

From benevolence, by which we will good to another, the affect of mercy arises, and this addresses a special difficulty and therefore requires a special virtue which takes its rise from charity. Mercy involves the tempering of sadness or of sorrow before an alien evil and looks to lift the neighbor from misery or defect (q. 30).

External effects of charity – In the following three questions, Saint Thomas discusses external effects of charity and mercy. The first is beneficence, which arises from benevolence, insofar as it effectively wills the good of another as such (q. 31). The second effect is almsgiving, which is an act of mercy that eases the bodily or spiritual misery of another (q. 32). One type of almsgiving gets special treatment, namely, fraternal correction. This does not involve an accusation based on justice or the rules of justice, which proceed from inquiry and denunciation, but, out of charity and so far as is possible without injury to the reputation and honor of the neighbor, seeks to correct him by dispensing the alms of correction. (If it took away his reputation for honor against his will it would be injustice, not almsgiving.) Of this and the order to be observed in it, Saint Thomas treats in q. 33.

c. Sins against Charity

Hatred of God, which is the worst and chief of vices, is directly opposed to the principal act of charity and thus maximally contrary to it. Nothing is less desirable or likely to move the will, for nothing is more contrary to love. It is not a capital vice from which others arise but rather the final and most profound point in which other vices terminate and is the sin proper to the damned (q. 34).

As for the vices opposed to the effects of charity, namely, joy, peace, and mercy: there are two vices opposed to joy, sloth (*accidia*) and envy. Charity rejoices in God and neighbor. Such joy is opposed by a disgust with God and divine things, insofar as boredom, distaste for divine things, invades the soul: Psalm 106, 18: "Their soul abhorred all food and they drew near to the gates of death." Also Psalm 118, 28, "My soul sheds tears in sorrow." This sadness, opposed to the divine good, is the special vice of which the Apostle speaks in 2 Corinthians 7, 10: "The sorrow that is according to the world produces death." It is therefore a mortal sin, since it is opposed to the divine good that had through charity, and it is a capital vice because a man falls into many sins in the effort to avoid being overcome by sadness and tedium (**q. 35**).

Envy is specifically opposed to the joy of charity insofar as it relates to one's neighbor. For although there are many ways in which we can feel sadness about another's good (as the Philosopher observes in 2 *Rhetoric* 9, 1386b), envy is the special sadness caused when another's good exceeds mine and results in inequality. Thus it most formally looks to the neighbor's good insofar as he is similar to me. It regards the good of another as the diminishment of my own good, not as if it actually took away what is mine (that would elicit fear rather than envy) but precisely because the other's increases and is no longer equal to mine, diminishing my good only relatively. Envy exists between similar and equal persons and pertains to pusillanimity or smallness of soul in one who, unable to increase his own glory, wants that of another to decrease to the level of his. Of itself it is a mortal and capital sin because its motive, one's own glory, is most desirable and causes many other things to be sought or avoided (**q. 36**).

Peace is the second effect of charity, and it implies union and tranquility, both of heart (and thus it is called concord) and of word and deed. To peace as concord, discord is opposed, of which Saint Thomas treats in **q. 37**. The opposite of peace as implying tranquility or calmness of speech is contention, which is a disordered and clamorous assault on truth (**q. 38**). To peace as it implies tranquillity in deed and work, four vices are opposed, namely, schism, war, strife, and sedition. These are distinct since schism impugns the unity of the Church, which is a unity of relation or order whereby all members are ordered under a principal head in heaven and his vicar on earth: it is the unity of charity because all members grow from the Holy Spirit "who prepares a home for the forlorn" (Psalm 67, 7), and this is called the communion of the saints, or of sanctity and charity. He who impugns the unity of order, unwilling to remain in union with its head, is schismatic. War implies contradiction and destroys unity between republic and republic; thus it belongs only to the prince and head of the republic who has the right to use the sword for the conservation of the whole community. Strife implies conflict between private persons of the same republic or community. Sedition, finally, is the dissolution of peace between parties in the same republic as when one group agitates against another. Of schism he treats in **q. 39**, of war in **q. 40**, of strife in **q. 41**, and of sedition in **q. 42**.

Third, mercy and beneficence are effects of charity, and many vices opposed to them are also opposed to virtues that are potential parts of justice, such as illiberality, ingratitude, etc., of which he will treat later. Scandal is opposed to beneficence as it specially arises from charity. Scandal is cause of the spiritual ruin of another by word and deed, something especially opposed to fraternal correction, which seeks the reparation of ruin. There are several forms of this: merely passive, that is, rising from the indisposition of the subject; malicious, the scandal of the Pharisees, which treats as scandalous what is no scandal; or as arising from the ignorance or infirmity of the subject, which is called the scandal of the little ones, which is not scandal in itself but only incidentally due to the indisposition of the subject. When, however, occasion for spiritual ruin not due to the indisposition of the subject is given, by the doing and act of the agent, it is called active scandal. And then if it is simply a consequence of an act which is otherwise sinful, but intended for some end other than spiritual ruin of the neighbor, scandal as such is done but not of a particular kind, and then it is only an aggravating circumstance. But if the ruin of another is intended as the per se object, then scandal will not attach incidentally to what is done, but constitute a special vice against the effect of charity (**q. 43**).

d. The Precepts of Charity

In the fourth part, Saint Thomas treats the precepts of charity, both as ordered to God and to neighbor, and how this precept is fulfilled in this life, and the like, in **q. 44**.

e. The Gift Corresponding to Charity

In the final part he treats of the gift corresponding to charity, namely, wisdom. This is essentially in intellect because it implies judgment concerning divine things through the highest cause, not only as involving assent to believed things (which pertains to faith), but a discretionary judgment through a kind of experience of the divine (which does not pertain to faith). It has its root and foundation in the will and charity, because to judge through the highest causes takes place in two ways. In one way from principles illumined and acquired by intellect, and this is the mode of human wisdom, which is not a gift. In another way by union and connaturality with the highest cause itself, God, as it were by taste and savor, as is said in Psalm 33, 9, "Taste and see," where sight arises from taste and savor. Therefore wisdom is called a sapid knowledge, much as one to whom chastity is connatural judges of chastity better than one who acquires [abstract] knowledge of chastity. He becomes connatural [akin] and conjoined to someone thanks to the highest cause by union through charity, according to 1 Corinthians 6, 17, "For he who cleaves to the Lord is one spirit with him" and Hiertheus in *On the Divine Names* is called "perfect in divine things, not as learning them, but as experiencing them." Such wisdom is a gift, because it "comes down from above," as is said in James 3, 17. Of this gift and of the corresponding beatitude, namely "Blessed are the peacemakers," since peace is tranquillity of order, and it pertains to wisdom to order, he treats in **q. 45**.

f. Sins Opposed to Gift

Because stupidity is opposed to the wisdom that arises from the purging of the heart and union with God, the particular cause of stupidity is corruption of heart, and thus is the daughter of luxury whose distinct effect is the dulling of the senses (**q. 46**).

b. The Cardinal Virtues
1. Prudence

Saint Thomas considers the cardinal virtues in his familiar way, more or less, adding only the treatment of the parts of these virtues (something he did not do in the case of the theological virtues), because the cardinal virtues, being principal ones, have other virtues under them as either potential or subjective parts.

There are five things to consider concerning prudence. First, prudence itself; second, its parts; third, the corresponding gift; fourth, the opposed vices; fifth, its precepts.

a. Prudence Itself

Saint Thomas treats the essence of prudence in a single question. There are two kinds of virtue in practical reason, namely, art and prudence, and art has for its object the make-able object, whereas prudence bears on what is to be done. These differ in that what is do-able is a voluntary or free act and therefore is directed not by certain and determinate rules as art is but by free and prudential ones. The make-able is called a work, an artifact, the nature of which is not arbitrary, but determined according to the rules of art. The chief praise of prudence, accordingly, lies in its application to things to be done, and its principal act is to command. For if one knows what ought to be done and does not act accordingly when he ought, he is imprudent, something that does not happen in the case of art, for one is not called a bad artisan if he does not apply his knowledge but only if he does not have the art. Thus it falls to prudence to direct voluntary or moral acts lest they fall short of rectitude in the individual application. It does not fall to prudence to rectify the will with regard to the intention of the end, therefore, but only choice and the selection of the means. The end and its rectitude are determined by nature. Prudence directs through *synderesis*, the grasp of first practical principles, which is, as it were, a habit and, as grasping first principles, is higher than prudence. But the means are not determined by nature as the end is but vary according to diverse circumstances. Therefore finding the fitting singular means that are right with respect to all circumstances is the work of correct discourse and a directing which applies to the here and now: that comes about through prudence. So it does not fall to prudence to determine and constitute the end, but rather, presupposing the right intention of the end, to determine and order the fitting means in the singular case. Because it presupposes the right intention in any matter, and this pertains to the virtues, Saint Thomas says that prudence presupposes all the moral virtues, not absolutely and perfectly, but each with respect to its own matter, for intention is directed by *synderesis*, not by prudence. But with respect to the ultimate perfection of virtue, which is the choice of the determinate means according to all the circumstances, this presupposes prudence and is directed by it (**q. 47**).

b. The Parts of Prudence

In each cardinal virtue three kinds of parts can be distinguished, namely, integral parts, subjective parts, and potential parts. Integral parts are constitutive of the integrity of a thing. Subjective parts are the species contained in a genus. Potential parts are the virtues or powers of a thing, each of which is adequate to the whole essence of the thing, but they look to their particular activity.

In the virtue of prudence, those perfections or dispositions which come together to constitute and make whole the act of prudence are called its integral parts. Saint Thomas distinguishes eight of them, namely, memory, reason, understanding, docility, ingenuity (*sollertia* which is also called *eustochia*), foresight, circumspection, and caution. The first five are ordered to knowing rightly both in counsel and in judgment, and thus they perfect *eubulia* (counsel) and *synesis* (judgment) which serve prudence. The other three are ordered to commanding rightly, and they perfect the chief act of prudence.

The subjective parts of prudence are the different species contained in it, which are distinguished by the different ways of governing and directing with respect to different ends: thus prudence is diversified into political, economic, military, and so on.

The potential parts are the virtues joined to prudence which look to its less principal acts, for of the virtues those are called cardinal or principal which look to the principal matter or act in its manner of regulating. But those which look to lesser matters or less difficult matters in the operation of the virtue are called less principal or potential. With respect to prudence, the chief and more difficult act is to command rightly; judging and taking counsel are lesser acts. Therefore *synesis* (judgement) and *eubulia* (counsel), and *gnome* (activity), which concern judgment and counsel, are secondary or less principal virtues of prudence.

He treats all these parts in common in **q. 48**, the integral parts in **q. 49**, the subjective parts in **q. 50**. There are four species of prudence, namely, ruling, which pertains to the prince, the political, which pertains to citizens that they might prudently obey; economic, which directs the family; military, which directs the army not simply in commanding soldiers but in expelling the enemy. The potential parts are treated in **q. 51**. These are *synesis* (judgment), *eubulia* (counsel), and *gnome* (acuity), because although the principal act of prudence is to command, the prudent man must also take counsel and judge what is to be done. These virtues overcome various difficulties, for there are some who take counsel well but judge badly, and vice versa. Good counsel pertains to *eubulia*, and good judgment about things to be done to *synesis*. That is why the Greeks called sensible folk *syneti* and their opposite *asyneti*. *Gnome*, however which is the same thing as perspicuity of judgment, implies judgment about things to be done in extraordinary cases and is moved by higher principles and is to *synesis* as wisdom is to knowledge.

c. Corresponding Gift of Prudence

The Gift of the Holy Spirit corresponding to prudence is the gift of counsel. It is called the gift of counsel rather than of prudence because the chief act of prudence is to command, which implies to move rather than to be moved. The Gifts of the Holy Spirit, however, make a man responsive to movement by the Holy Spirit rather than moving, and this is why it is called the gift of counsel rather than prudence (**q. 52**).

d. The Vices Opposed to Prudence

Some vices are opposed to prudence because of a defect, others because of excess. Those involving a defect make a man imprudent, whereas those which are excessive go beyond prudence, such as shrewdness (*astutia*), fraud (*dolus*), over solicitude (*nimia sollicitudo*), etc. He treats the vices due to defect in **q. 53**, namely, imprudence, lack of consideration, temerity, inconstancy, and so forth, which are opposed to prudence and its parts. He gives special attention to negligence which is opposed to solicitude and destroys prudence in a special way, namely, by omission or remission (**q. 54**). As for those vices arising from excess that are opposed to prudence and solicitude, they either direct means to a bad end, and are called the prudence of the flesh, or regard some good or bad end using depraved ways or means, such as shrewdness, fraud, and excessive concern for the future (**q. 55**).

e. The Precepts of Prudence

There is no special precept of the Decalogue concerning prudence because its precepts express what is immediately deduced from the most universal principles. In the Law of the Gospel, which is the law of perfection and therefore requires a man to be instructed, a precept of prudence is given in Matthew 10, 16: "Be ye wise as serpents . . ." (**q. 56**).

2. Justice

The treatise on justice is lengthy, extending from q. 57 through q. 122, because there are so many potential parts included under it. Saint Thomas does not deal with opposed vices separately but mentions them as he discusses each virtue contained under justice. There are four main headings in the treatise on justice. First, justice itself; second, its parts, subjective, integral, and potential; third, the corresponding gift; fourth, the precepts of justice.

a. Justice Itself

Proceeding according to the order of doctrine, he explains first the formal specifying object of justice, then the habit or virtue, which is the thing specified, and the opposed vice which is injustice, ending with its proper act, which is to render (*reddere*) to each what is his. The object of justice is the right (*jus*) or the just, since justice looks to this as to its object. Of right and its diversity, as in natural law, the law of nations, and positive law, and other like things, he treats in **q. 57**.

As for the habit specified, the virtue of justice, Saint Thomas considers its definition, namely, that it is a habit inclining the will, a constant and permanent will to give to each his due. So he considers its subject, the will. Because it is ordered to another and thus proceeds rationally and not merely on the basis of what is sensed, and because it respects the debt to be rendered or given, it does not perfect knowledge but the will which inclines toward giving. He then considers the dignity of justice which is higher than those moral virtues which are concerned with passions. This is especially true of legal justice which respects the common good, or legal obligation; and is architectonically or principally in the prince who orders and governs the common good, but ministerially and subjectively it is in the governed who obey him (**q. 58**).

He treats the vice of injustice in **q. 59**, showing how it is opposed to the special virtue justice is. Of its very kind, it is a mortal sin, because it is against the good of the other, the neighbor, to whom harm comes from it. So it is against charity too, which loves the good of the neighbor.

As for the act of justice, he shows that it is twofold: first, to render to each what is his, which belongs, as it were, to execution, and second, to determine or judge equality and proportion among these things, and this is called a mean in the thing (*medium rei*) as opposed to the mean of reason which also pertains to the other virtues insofar as they look to the regulation of acts proceeding from the will insofar as they do so proceed. Justice not only imposes the judgment of reason on the very act of will, but also determines equality and proportion between things or persons, not that justice elicits the act of judgment, which is an act of knowledge (and is in fact an act of *synesis*, which is a part of prudence), but justice disposes the will in such a way that intellect is fittingly moved to judge (**q. 60**).

b. The Parts of Justice

The second thing to be discussed is the matter of justice, namely, its parts.

1. Subjective Parts

And first its subjective parts, that is, the species of justice:

legal, distributive, and commutative. Justice consists in an order or relation to another which can be considered either as part to part, that is, between two private persons, or as whole to part or, conversely, of part to whole. The former is commutative justice; the latter distributive, insofar as there is a fitting distribution to the parts by the chief of the republic; the third is legal justice, whereby a person respects the common good and legal obligation. He sets aside legal justice, because he treated it in q. 58, where he spoke of the dignity of justice insofar as it is not concerned with a particular debt but commonly with what is owed by all the virtues, from which the common good coalesces. Here he discusses only the other two species where a particular obligation or mean is involved. Distributive justice aims at one kind of equality, commutative at another. For distributive justice seeks an equality of proportionality between the person with and the thing distributed to him, what is called a geometric equality. Commutative justice aims at an equality of thing to thing, as in exchanges and contracts, what is called arithmetic equality. Of these two he speaks in **q. 61.**

Just Acts

After discussing its species, he takes up the principal acts of justice. The act of distributive justice is perfected in a judgment by which the distribution of goods is discerned. He has discussed judgment in q. 60. The act of commutative justice is to render to a particular person what is his due. This comes about in two ways. First, by reason of some action of voluntary exchange, as in various contracts, or secondly because of an involuntary action, such as injury or harm, which requires restitution. The first could only be adequately discussed in terms of all contracts, something that is not the task of the theologian, save insofar as they are done licitly or illicitly, and in this way it is best treated under the heading of the sins opposed to justice. As for the second, restitution, he takes that up in **q. 62.**

Unjust Acts

Next he discusses the vices opposed to these two species of

justice. First, he discusses the sin opposed to distributive justice, which takes into account personal status in the sense that it is based on the condition of the person and not on the proportion required of the good distributed (**q. 63**).

The vices opposed to commutative justice are many and occupy him through q. 78. They can be ordered as follows. Commutative justice concerns the exchange of things. Such exchanges can come about with the consent and will of both parties, or with one unwilling or suffering and then they are involuntary.

Injustice by involuntary exchange can arise from deed or word. From deeds, either with respect to a given person, with respect to someone related, or with respect to things possessed. If in the first way, there can be the injury of homicide (**q. 64**), or of bad treatment, as through mutilation, beatings, sequestration, etc. (**q. 65**). Injury to a person connected to oneself can involve a spouse, as in adultery, or against a child, as by violation or incest: these he treats when he takes up the species of dissipation (*luxuria*). As for things owned, there can be injury when one takes another's goods against his will; when done secretly, this is theft, when done openly by violence, it is robbery (*rapina*) (**q. 66**).

Injury by word can be done in or out of court. Saint Thomas lists five ways in which injury can be done in court, and five ways in which it can be done out of court. In court there are five people involved: the judge, the accuser, the witness, the accused, and the advocate. Injury done by the judge is discussed in **q. 67**; sin on the side of the accuser is discussed in **q. 68**; on the side of the guilty, and justice and injustice in his regard, in **q. 69**. Injury on the part of the witness in **q. 70**, and on the part of the advocate in **q. 71**. To these the sins and injustices of other ministers of justice can be reduced.

Similarly outside of court a judgment can do injury by way of words or other external signs which make known the faults of another, and this in five ways: contumely, gossip, denigration, derision, and malediction. These differ as follows. Contumely dishonors another by disclosing some moral fault, as that he is a heretic or thief, or a non-moral evil, outrageously calling him stunted or impoverished, or by calling attention to the things one has done for him (this is reproach). All these are included under contumely (**q. 72**). Gossip does not dishonor totally, but takes away from another's reputation (**q. 73**). Denigration is saying evil of one's neighbor, sowing discord (**q. 74**). Derision or mockery manifests some evil or defect of another in order to cause him shame and cover him with confusion (**q. 75**). Finally, malediction discloses some evil, not by affirming it, but implying it (**q. 76**). These are the sins of injustice that arise from involuntary exchanges or actions.

As for voluntary exchanges, which take place with consent and by contract, there are only two chief sins, fraud and usury. Fraud concerns buying and selling or other exchanges which resemble buying, such as renting, hiring, associating, negotiating, and the like, and is sin and injustice in those activities. Usury takes place in borrowing or any contract which is like borrowing, at least virtually with an eye to anticipated profit (**q. 78**). Aside from theft, rapine, fraud, and usury there are no other species of sin in voluntary exchanges.

2. Integral Parts

Having discussed its subjective parts, he goes on to discuss the integral parts of justice which are not parts entitatively making it up but certain conditions or dispositions concurrent with the integral perfection of justice, which is to do good and avoid evil. First, as seen from the side of the agent insofar as he performs a good act, that is, one arising in a good way from the agent himself. Second, good comes about from the external thing insofar as equality or inequality are established in it, and thus the good and the just are the same. The first way to do good and avoid evil is common to all the virtues, and there are two parts of it, not one and the same movement, avoidance of evil involving a *term from which*, and doing good approaching the *term to which*. To do good is to establish equality and to avoid evil is not to cause harm. These differ since he who does the one does not do the other, since it is one thing not to wound and another to pay a debt, the one is violated by omission, the other by commission (**q. 79**).

3. Potential Parts

The potential parts of justice are many and various. First Saint Thomas speaks of them in general, then specifically. By the potential parts of a virtue he means those habits or virtues which agree with the principal virtue in the way they tend toward and regard the object, but differ in their matter. The cardinal or principal virtue looks rather to the principal or more difficult matter, whereas its potential parts bear on a less difficult matter or lend their mode to the principal virtue. The notion of justice consists in this: that what is owed another is given him according to equality. Hence the principal note of justice is saved in that matter in which a difficult debt is paid and the equality is also hard to attain. Where the note of difficulty is less prominent but the note of being owed remains and equality is brought about differently, there is a lesser matter and a potential part of justice. Principal potential parts of justice are distinguished when there is a variation in the thing owed and in the equality demanded. Some look to a difficult debt owed to another, but they do not save equality in rendering it; others on the contrary establish equality but do not have a difficult debt or legal one, that is, something imposed by law, but rather a moral one thanks to the intrinsic good (*bonum honestum*) of virtue.

In the first category are put those virtues which render what is owed to God, parents, and superiors, or more excellent men; we are maximally obliged to such persons, but we cannot establish equality with them. Religion is the potential part of justice which looks to God; piety, which looks to parents; observance, with respect to superiors.

In the second category the moral debt or that of honor (*honestitatis*) is considered in two ways. In one way when the honorableness of virtue cannot be saved without it, because it is a question of a debt between men, and this is threefold. On the side of the one owing there is veracity so that it proceeds without mendacity or pretense; on the side of the one owed, recompense, which causes gratitude in a man when goods are involved and vindication in the case of evils. In another way the debt is considered, not as absolutely required to preserve the honor (*honestas*) of virtue but that it might be better preserved: two virtues are concerned with this, namely liberality and affability or friendship. He treats of these in general in **q. 80**. They are treated in particular in the following questions.

He treats of the first potential part of justice, which is religion, in **q. 80**, where there are three things to be taken up. First, the essence of religion, second, its different acts which look to different matter, third, the opposed vices.

As for the essence of religion and the way it is distinguished from the theological and moral virtues, and its perfection, he treats in **q. 81**.

The acts of religion are many and various by reason of the diverse matter which is assumed in the divine cult; thus they are not distinguished in the formal notion of the virtue but according to matter in much the same way as in a man we distinguish heterogeneous parts materially, not formally. Religion submits to God and his worship both spiritual and interior things and the bodily and external. On the part of interior offering we either subject our will by prompt and attentive application in doing the things which are of God, and this is devotion (if this is done by delivering oneself over to him by a solemn promise it is a vow). He treats of devotion in **q. 82**. Or we subject the intellect by lifting the mind to God, and this is prayer, which he treats in **q. 83**.

The acts offered to God in external worship are either done by subjecting or ordering something to divine worship, or by reverently ordering something to him. In the first way we can subject our own body or the things we possess to divine worship. When we subject the body this is adoration, which he treats in **q. 84**. If we subject our possessions, we do so either by renouncing them or by promising and fulfilling our promise. Renunciation of goods is done by turning them over to the honor of God and to profess his supreme excellence, and this is done by sacrifice, treated in **q. 85**. Or we offer them to sustain God's ministers, and are such simple offers as first fruits or tithes. Saint Thomas treats offerings in **q. 86** and tithes in **q. 87**. If we promise ourselves or our things to God, there is a vow, which is an act of religion, because it is made out of reverence for God. This can happen in two ways, either by a bare promise, and then it is a simple vow. When in addition there is a handing over or consecrating of the thing promised and the acceptance by the Church in the name of God, there is a solemn vow, because a thing to be solemnized demands to be fulfilled and completed, although the Church can make one a religious and accept one into the religious state by a bare promise in the simple vow, and not by the consecration of the one vowing as well. These are treated in **q. 88**.

We can also, out of religious respect for God, assume something divine, whose authority we interpose, and use the divine name to signify God's authority. This name can be used in divine worship in three ways. First, to confirm the truth already infallibly known by God, we invoke him as witness to show the truth which we affirm as certain; this affirmation belongs to the worship of God because thus we profess that God is the highest truth. To do this is to swear (**q. 89**). Secondly, we use the divine name, not to confirm truth and oblige ourselves to its certitude, but to extract the truth from another by the invocation of God's name, and this is adjuring, as we compel the demons by adjuring or to plead with men (**q. 90**) Finally, we use the divine name to praise him and invoke his aid, and this is invocation (**q. 91**).

He turns next to the sins opposed to religion, some of which are opposed to it due to excess and others due to defect. Superstition is opposed by excess, irreligion by defect. He treats superstition first in general and then its species. The general treatment is found in **q. 92**, where he shows that superstition is a superfluity in divine worship, not of true worship, of which there cannot be too much, but in things which do not belong to true worship. The species of superstition are distinguished according to two principles. Either the true God is worshiped but in an unfitting way, or worship is given to a false god, some creature thought to be God. He treats superstition of the first kind in **q. 93**. The second kind is treated in three questions according to the subspecies of it. For worship involves both the person to whom it is given and the signs of divinity he exhibits. If one is mistaken about the person, offering worship to a creature rather than to God, there is idolatry (**q. 94**). If one is mistaken about the signs indicative of divinity, he can err in two ways since the signs and ceremonies by which we worship God are either ordered to our instruction, that we might be taught by God, as through readings, prayers, sacraments, and so forth, or they are ordered to directing our acts by observing what God has instituted. Divination, which seeks to be instructed by the devil, hoping to know something from him by express or tacit invocation, goes against the first principle (q. 95). The different ways in which divination asks something of the devil are necromancy, augury, discovery of gold (*aurspicium*), the study of the stars, the lines of the hand, and other like ways. To the second principle is opposed superstitious observances, such as the wearing of talismans, scriptural texts suspended from the neck to which one attributes a magic efficacy, and the like, not only to know the future, which is divination, but to bring about certain effects, such as health, the discovering of gold, the acquiring of knowledge, and so forth. Of such superstition he treats in q. 96.

The vice of irreligion, contempt or irreverence for God, is opposed to religion by defect. Irreverence can occur with respect to God himself or to sacred things dedicated to his worship. There are two kinds of irreverence toward God himself, one against his very excellence, the other against his name. The first consists in detracting from his honor by idolatry, already discussed, or lessening his honor by doubting him in some way, putting to the test his power or knowledge, that is, tempting God (q. 97). Irreverence for the name of God takes place in perjury or swearing falsely (q. 98). As for sacred things, irreverence toward them is shown by violating their holiness or exchanging them for temporal things. The first is sacrilege, which can come about in many ways: by irreverence to persons consecrated to God or to sacred places or to things bearing holiness, like the sacraments or relics of the saints (q. 99). The second kind of irreverence is simony, which is also opposed to religion, and he treats this in q. 100.

After religion and among the potential parts of justice which have a rigorous debt but do not involve equality, there is piety, which renders a debt to parents, fatherland, or relatives who require a special subjection because from parents and country we have the principle of our existence and governance, though in a manner less than from God. We cannot repay equally because we cannot give them what they have given us. He discusses piety in q. 101.

The third potential virtue of justice which renders a rigorous debt but does not involve equality, respects princes or persons of established excellence who are the principle of our governance but not of our existence. The virtue cultivating such excellence is called observance, which is treated first in general (q. 102), then in its two species, subservience (*dulia*) and obedience (qq. 103–104). Subservience is distinguished from obedience by the manner of observance, because subservience implies service and inferiority to another as to a master, and especially signifies the observance we give the saints, who are particularly honorable lords because of their participation in divinity. By obedience we venerate a superior in his precepts and thus it is a special virtue exhibiting veneration to one commanding. If it meant only execution of precepts it would be relevant to all virtues which involve precepts. As for disobedience, [this] is the sin opposed to obedience, and particularly so when, out of contempt for the command, it takes away veneration for the superior – the very point of obedience (q. 105).

After these potential virtues, which involve a rigorous debt but not equality, there follow others of another class, those which establish equality but do not have a strict or legal debt, only the honorableness (*honestas*) of virtue. We find two orders here: some virtues without which the honorableness of virtue cannot be preserved in human society and others ordered to the better preservation of that debt. There are three virtues in the first category, namely, gratitude, vindication, and veracity; there are two in the second category, affability and liberality. Saint Thomas treats the first three in this order: first, gratitude and the vice opposed to it; second, vindication; third, veracity and the vices opposed to it. In preserving the debt of *honestas*, either obligation arises from some action which others do toward us, and we are held to recompense them, whether it involves good or evil, or it arises from our-selves and not for the sake of recompensing things done for us: such is veracity.

Therefore to recompense the debt arising from benefits conferred upon us, which do not involve a strict or legal debt as contracts do, but a gratuitous and honorable one, gratitude is required (**q. 106**). Its opposed vice is ingratitude, which happens when we omit to give thanks for a benefit received, or return evil for good. Of this he treats in **q. 107**. Recompense for evils, that is, to repress the harm brought, stop the perpe-trator from harming, and securing the relief of others, is the task of the virtue of vindication (**q. 108**), not only by imped-ing such an evil as present in the perpetrator (as by fraternal correction) since it is harmful to me or others following the demands of human society. The public person impedes it because of his office according to legal justice, the private per-son by the honorableness of virtue, either by defending him-self or by having recourse to a magistrate (**q. 109**).

Four vices are opposed to veracity. A lie is its contradicto-ry by means of words and hypocrisy by deeds. Dissembling is also opposed to veracity. He treats lying in **q. 110**, hypocrisy in **q. 111**. Each can come about in two ways, either by extolling oneself above what one is, or by pretending to be less. The first is boasting (*jactantia*), **q. 112**, the second irony, **q. 113**.

Finally, among the potential parts of justice are virtues ordered to the preserving the debt of honor and decency. Not absolutely, but for the better. Affability and liberality are ordered to this: affability is ordered to our living with others pleasantly as it is fitting we do, both in word and deed. That there is a kind of debt of honor, although it is not one in the strict legal sense, is discussed in **q. 114**. Two vices are opposed to these, one by excess, namely, adulation, when one finds liv-ing with another so delightful that one wishes to please him even when something evil is involved (he treats this in **q. 115**). The other vice arises from defect, namely, argumentativeness (*litigium*), when someone wants to contradict another not from a defect in love uniting souls (for then it would belong to discord), but because he is hard on him in conversing and saddens him; thus the debt of human society is removed. He treats this in **q. 116**. Another virtue, liberality, seems especially distant from the notion of strict justice, because it does not give to another his due but what belongs to the giver; still it preserves something of debt according to honor and the decency of virtue, insofar as it is an obligation of human society to give things to others. One does so not only out of compassion for another's misery (which belongs to mercy), but even when there is no question of misery. That is why liberality does not posit equality between two things, but bestows on another what is fitting to the nature of the giver and the one bequeathing. It pertains to it, therefore, to compose appetite with respect to the things it uses, what we generally call money, such that one does not so seek money that he is unwilling to part with it and give it when this is fitting in human society. It moderates the concupiscible passions concerning what is given and gotten according as they lead to the obligation (*debitum*) and decency of this society. Hence it is not in the first place and as such the moderating of concupiscible passions but the rendering of a debt. Magnificence however which turns on great possessions which have the note of difficulty rather than duty, pertains to fortitude. He treats of liberality in **q. 117**. Two vices are opposed to it, one by way of defect, namely, avarice, which is the inordinate love of possessions or money, and not giving it up even when the demands of human society require it. The possession of things is most desirable since men ardently desire a sufficiency of them, this being one of the conditions of happiness. Avarice is a capital vice because it can serve as motive and end by which a man either does or does not avoid many other things. He treats avarice in **q. 118**. Prodigality is opposed to it by way of excess, which overflows in the desire to give, when and where it is not required. He treats this in **q. 119**.

Besides all these potential virtues of justice, and subject parts, which look to particular justice, there remains to treat a virtue connected with legal justice, one called equity (*epicheia*), which is ordered to the observance of law in some extraordinary case, in which if one held to the strict letter of the law he would depart from rectitude. Equity dictates that one ought not at a given time attend to the letter of the law but to what the law would intend if it had taken into account a given case. Law cannot embrace every case in particular and if it is defective in anything equity dictates what is to be done, not according to the letter of the law, but according to its equity. Just as law universally dictates that borrowed items should be returned, in the case of the enraged owner seeking his sword, equity dictates that it not be given over. Therefore equity corrects law with respect to its universality, namely when the law would become iniquitous if it were observed universally in all cases no matter the result. He treats this in **q. 120.**

c. The Corresponding Gift

There remains to treat of the corresponding gift, which is piety. Alone of the Gifts of the Holy Spirit, piety involves what is owed to another, considering God as father, and all the faithful as brothers according to the spirit of adoption. Under this formality he covers universally everything which involves the note of debt. He treats this gift in **q. 121.**

d. The Precepts of Justice

The last thing to be considered under justice are the precepts which are given concerning it. All the precepts of justice are contained in the Decalogue whose precepts involve another, whether God or neighbor. The first three precepts pertain to God; the fourth to the debt of piety toward parents; the other six prohibit injuries to other persons; consequently, concupiscence is especially prohibited with respect to adultery and theft, which relate to another, the venereal being most desirable and money having the note of greatest usefulness. Concupiscence in their regard is accordingly specially prohibited. He treats these in **q. 122.**

3. Fortitude

The third cardinal virtue is fortitude to which, as he did with the other virtues, following the proper order of treatment, Saint Thomas devotes four principal chapters. First, he explains the nature of fortitude, its act, and the opposed vices.

Second, its parts. Third, the gift corresponding to it. Fourth, its precepts.

a. Fortitude Itself

On the question of the nature of fortitude, he discusses both its subject and its object, that is, the matter with which it is concerned.

Its subject is the irascible sense appetite, although a virtue's acts of choice are properly and directly in will, which is a deliberative and elective faculty. Nevertheless, because choice cannot be correctly made when it is impeded by immoderate passions, there is need of a virtue in sense appetite to order the passions in such a way that the correct choice of will can be made, impediments having been removed. Since there is a twofold appetite, one concupiscible, the other irascible, temperance is needed to moderate passion in the concupiscible, and fortitude in the irascible. He treats fortitude first as the nobler insofar as it moderates the irascible which bears on what is arduous.

1. The Matter of Fortitude

Its objects or matter, mediated and remote, are perils and labors, and not just any, but those which are greatest, because a man ought to make firm the good of reason and virtue against all perils, lest he ever depart from reason. Above all, he ought to handle the greatest perils, since one firm in their regard will easily handle lesser ones. A person who contemns the greatest perils, as in war where there is the danger of death, will be called absolutely brave. The immediate objects or matter of fortitude are the passions of fear and boldness: only perils that are feared can cause will to retreat. Fortitude removes the impediment of immoderate fear and also restrains excessive boldness, lest one be led into perils without necessity. He treats the nature of fortitude's act in a general way, in **q. 123**. Of its most perfect act, martyrdom which is elicited by fortitude and commanded by charity, and of what is required for martyrdom or is consequent on it, he treats in **q. 124**.

2. Vices Opposed to Fortitude

Having explained the nature and act of fortitude, he turns to the vices opposed to it. Since fortitude turns on fear and audacity or boldness, one tends to sin in this area either out of fear or audacity, and in both either by excess or defect. Immoderate fear is opposed to fortitude when one unreasonably refuses to expose himself to peril. He treats such fear in **q. 125**. Impassiveness is opposed to it by way of excess, when one does not fear, even when there is a rational reason for fearing. He treats this in **q. 126**.

Similarly, with respect to audacity, excessive and insufficient boldness are opposed to fortitude. For as the Philosopher says (3 *Ethic.* 10, 1116a): "while in these situations they display confidence, they do not hold their ground against what is really terrible." Hence through excess there is immoderate boldness when one flies against all counsel and reason. By defect when one even after taking counsel does not dare to act with constancy. Since this usually comes about because of fear, which dampens boldness, it is not given as a vice distinct from fear, although it is probable that a peculiar vice opposite to boldness through defect should be recognized, called disheartedness, namely when one not out of fear but from a defect of hope, not hoping that he would follow through, does not dare, although he does not fear. Of audacity he treats in **q. 127**.

b. The Parts of Fortitude

Saint Thomas first gives a general account of the parts of fortitude and then goes on to discuss them in particular.

In the general account, three kinds of parts are distinguished, namely, subjective, integral, and potential, although he says nothing of the subjective, since fortitude has none because of the limited matter over which it ranges, namely, maximum peril, mortal peril. Because of the nature of maximum peril it does not admit division into species.

1. Integral Parts

Saint Thomas distinguishes the integral parts of fortitude on the basis of two acts, to attack or to endure. There are four virtues which strengthen the soul in attack and endurance. Attack involves arduous things, which pertain to fortitude alone: magnificence deals with doing great things; not doubting victory, magnanimity fills the soul with confidence in victory. In enduring, the soul is strengthened with respect to two things, namely, [patience] with respect to the greatness of the evil for the one sustaining it and perseverance with respect to how long and continuous it is. Now these two acts are in the concupiscible which moderates sadness, but they are called integral parts of fortitude, which is in the irascible, because the irascible arises from the concupiscible and thus these have reverberations in the irascible.

2. Potential Parts

The potential parts of fortitude are these same four virtues when they turn on matters distinct from the principal matter of fortitude. That is, when they are concerned with mortal peril and other maximum dangers involving attack and endurance, these virtues have the force of integral parts of fortitude, but with regard to other matters, for example, expense, honors, bad fortune, and so on, these virtues are potential parts of fortitude, their names remaining the same. In much the same way, the intellectual and sensitive are potential parts of the rational soul, but they are species or grades of living things. These parts are discussed in **q. 128**.

Moving to the particular account of the potential parts of fortitude, which are the four virtues mentioned, namely, magnanimity and magnificence, which correspond to attack or aggression in matters other than mortal peril, and patience and perseverance which involve the act of enduring in less than maximal perils.

He first takes up magnanimity which looks to great honor or those deeds on which great honor can follow. In order to be a virtue, magnanimity should not look directly to the honor, but to that on which it follows, because true honor follows on virtue alone, as a testimony to it. Hence it ought not be sought for its own sake, insofar as it is public testimony, but rather the virtue on which it follows is to be sought. Magnanimity moderates aggression in the hope for high honor, lest a man should be too taken with honor or should want it for itself and not by reason of virtue or should want it disproportionately. Thus it strengthens the soul so that it tends to things worthy of honor in a proportionate way, and is most compatible with humility, which represses the soul with respect to undeserved honor out of consideration of one's defects. Although any virtue can deal with the little or great in its subject matter, magnanimity in these same virtues seeks the magnitude of the deed, not simply as a condition of it, but as involving a special formal note of the difficult to be won by attack. He discusses magnanimity in **q. 129**.

He treats of vices opposed to magnanimity in the following questions. Three vices are opposed to magnanimity by way of excess, namely, presumption, ambition, and vainglory; by way of defect, pusillanimity. They are distinguished in this way: magnanimity looks to great deeds with the moderation of due proportion, honor following on the great deed, and glory as the effect of honor. Presumption is opposed to magnanimity with reference to the great deed, for it tends to it without proportion. Ambition concerns the consequent honor, inordinately desiring an undeserved honor precisely in order to be honored. Vainglory is opposed to magnanimity as it concerns glory which is an effect of honor and has been defined as "being known to be illustrious and consequently praised." Vainglory seeks to be illustrious but is unfounded in deserved honor. When excessively sought as an end this is a capital vice. He discusses presumption in **q. 130**; ambition in **q. 131**; and vainglory in **q. 132**. Pusillanimity, the vice opposed to magnanimity by way of defect, when one refuses to seek what is due and proportioned to him, is treated in **q. 133**.

The second potential virtue of fortitude is magnificence, which looks to great external works that are properly called things to be made much as magnanimity concerns great things to be done that pertain to virtue or expansion of the soul. Every difficulty involved in making great external works comes from the cost, that is, money. Thus liberality is ordered to giving money for things to be made. Since money is given by way of a gift and a gift pertains especially to love, it falls to liberality chiefly to moderate the love of money and to elicit the love of giving. So too it falls to the magnificent man to provide great expense for external works, not under the note of giving, but under those of the great and arduous, which require aggression and fortitude, not regarding mortal peril, but regarding expenses and external costs. Therefore its act is not in the concupiscible as concerned with the love of giving money, but in the irascible under the note of expending and the cost of making great things, although it presupposes that the love of money has been moderated since otherwise this would impede expenditure on great works. He treats this virtue in **q. 134.**

He treats the vices opposed to magnificence in **q. 135.** They are two, one by way of defect, namely meanness, which intends only the smallness of expenditure and does not dare anything great. The other by way of excess, the Greek term for which is *banausia* and the Latin *consumptio*, which squanders money without reason or limit.

After magnanimity and magnificence, which are potential parts of fortitude on the part of the act of aggression, he treats two others which correspond to the act of enduring, namely, patience and perseverance. Patience endures evils insofar as they involve difficulty on the part of their very severity, or the greatness of the evil as such, short of mortal peril, which is the principal matter of fortitude; patience as a potential part of it must turn on other more common evils. It pertains to patience, accordingly, to moderate sudden sadness, strengthening the soul lest it succumb. This is not true of other virtues which concern sadness in their various domains, such as penitence and mercy, eliciting it as moderated. Patience however strengthens the soul even in their case lest it succumb to them, much as continence deters the soul lest it succumb to concupiscence, and in this is distinguished from temperance which moderates it as such. Thus patience pertains to the concupiscible by reason of the sadness against which it strengthens the soul. It is probable, however, that it does not reside in sense appetite itself, but in the will, which it strengthens to resist sadness, just as continence resides in it to resist concupiscence. Patience is discussed in **q. 136**.

The last potential virtue of fortitude, concerning the act of sustaining, is perseverance, which looks to the endurance of evil insofar as it has a special difficulty from the very duration of the act. For although duration seems a circumstance of the deed, still insofar as it causes a special difficulty in enduring evils it alters the nature of the motive and requires a special virtue. Thus just as patience moderates sadness arising from the severity of a present evil, so perseverance moderates fears of weariness or of some defect due to the duration of impending evil. Thus it is in the irascible appetite and a potential part of fortitude because it strengthens the soul against the difficulty arising from the duration of an evil and not from mortal peril. If perseverance lasts to the end, it is fulfilled, both from the side of choice and from that of execution. But if someone should have the purpose and chooses to persevere, he already has the act of the virtue of perseverance, although choice be impeded, because this is not from our choice, but from the pure help of divine grace. He treats this virtue in **q. 137**.

There are two vices opposed to perseverance, namely, through a defect, softness, and through excess, pertinacity. One is called soft who easily gives up, but one vanquished by great passions is not called soft because even the bravest cede things to great contraries. The one called soft gives in to small passions or frights, especially when he gives up only because of the deprivation of pleasure, since the lack of pleasure is but a weak motive. Therefore one who does not endure difficulties because he cannot for long forego pleasure is called soft. The pertinacious fellow is so called because he is unfittingly firm in his own opinion, and for this reason will not refuse to sustain long-term evil. He is opposed by way of excess to perseverance, although what is the cause of pertinacity, namely, delighting too much in one's own intended victory and adhesion to one's own opinion, is similar to the soft man who desires pleasures too much and cannot bear their absence. He speaks of these vices in **q. 138**.

c. The Corresponding Gift

Having explained the parts of fortitude, he treats of the gift corresponding to it, which is called the gift of fortitude, by which one is moved by the Holy Spirit to sustain or face certain arduous matters, which exceed human capacity, relying on divine help alone. Of this gift and the beatitude corresponding to it ("Blessed are they who hunger and thirst for justice"), which is very arduous, he speaks in **q. 139.**

d. The Precepts of Fortitude

Finally, he treats the precepts of fortitude and its parts, by which we are commanded to be brave and act manfully, in **q. 140.**

4. Temperance

Saint Thomas treats this virtue under three principal headings. First, he discusses the virtue of temperance and the vices opposed to it. Second, its parts, which are many and various. Third, the precepts given concerning it. He does not speak of the Gift of the Holy Spirit corresponding to it because, as he says in q. 141, a. 1, ad 3, no gift directly and primarily answers to temperance, although the gift of fear secondarily restrains carnal pleasures, according to Psalm 118, 120: "My flesh shudders with fear of thee." But fear primarily and as such shows reverence to God, by fearing his power and from this follows shuddering concern carnal matters, when one because of such fear does not dare burst out against God.

a. Temperance Itself and Vices Opposed to Temperance

On the first point, then, Saint Thomas discusses the very nature of temperance, supposing that our passions are of two kinds, some which flee evils and others which follow on the desire of the good. In fleeing evils, there is no peril except from some adjunct, as when one avoids evil to such an extent that he fails to do some reasonable good. Hence the virtues which reduce passions to a mean act chiefly to confirm the soul in the good lest it set it aside in order to flee an evil. The passions by which we tend toward sensible goods by their very vehemence and excess lead us away from pursuing the good of reason, such that retreat from the good of reason arises from excessive pursuit of sensible things. Experience tells us that great desire softens and weakens the heart. That is why it is necessary for the virtue which reduces such passions to a mean to restrain and cut off their immoderate growth. That is what temperance does, since its proper role is to restrain and establish a modification in the passions which pursue such sensible goods as pleasures.

But since to a principal or cardinal virtue there corresponds the more difficult and chief matter in its sphere, that is what must be assigned to the cardinal virtue of temperance. Among all sensible goods those pleasures are most vehement which are most natural, for nature especially inclines and tends to its own conservation with regard to both species and individual, but especially to the preservation of the species which is a more universal good and is presupposed by the individual. The venereal is connected to the preservation of the species as food is to the preservation of the individual, and their pleasures pertain to touch because although food is also sensed by taste with respect to flavor (as well as by smell with respect to aroma and sight with respect to beauty), still as nourishing it pertains to touch alone, for we are nourished by the warm and cold, dry and moist, which is why the Philosopher says that the sense of touch is the sense of food. Thus temperance, which is a cardinal virtue, has for its matter the pleasures of touch concerning which it is most difficult to refrain. He explains this in **q. 141**.

He treats of the vices opposed to temperance in **q. 142**. They are two: through defect, intemperance, which inordinately desires the pleasures of touch and wallows in them; through excess, what is called insensibility, when one flees the ordered use of sensible things.

b. The Parts of Temperance

On the second point, namely, the parts of temperance, he first gives a general treatment and then goes on to the particular treatment.

Generally, then, he distinguishes three kinds of parts – integral, subjective, and potential.

The integral parts are modesty and honor by which temperance is opposed to baseness, modesty by fleeing baseness, honor by loving its opposite. The movements regulated by temperance are especially base because most bestial.

There are two subjective parts, namely, chastity and abstinence, chastity moderating the venereal, abstinence moderating the pleasures of food. Shame serves chastity by moderating outward signs and chastity moderates sexual pleasure itself. Abstinence is divided into sobriety, which governs immoderation in drink, and abstinence with respect to food.

The potential parts are those virtues which moderate excess of passions or inclination in other matters than the pleasures of touch. Some moderate the will, such as continence, which restrains the will lest it succumb to stormy passions, others moderate the irascible, as wrath is moderated by mildness and clemency; humility moderates excessive boldness, or the hope which is directed toward one's own excellence. Others govern the things pertaining to external make-up, such as modesty and others which are reduced to modesty (q. 143).

1. Integral Parts

Having explained the parts of temperance in a general way, he goes on to a particular discussion of them.

And first the integral parts, namely, modesty and honor, by which a man especially shuns baseness. He treats modesty first, whereby one fears to be confused or tested by the base. It differs from penance because penance grieves for sin as such as offensive to God, but modesty flees the baseness of sin insofar as it fears its dishonor and disorder. Thus this does not pertain to the perfect man, nor is it a virtue, but rather a laudable passion, since it does not directly seek the good but flees evil because of the dishonor of it. Thus modesty is not a component part of temperance, but disposes to it. He treats modesty in q. 144. Of honor (*honestas*), by which one loves the beauty of virtue, not only in general (for thus every virtue is honorable or worthy of honor) but in particular insofar as it excludes baseness, which arises from desire for the base thing, as the Apostle observes: "And those we think the less honorable members of the body, we surround with more abundant honor, and our uncomely parts receive a more abundant comeliness." 1 Corinthians 12, 23. He treats this in **q. 145**.

2. Subjective Parts

As for the subjective parts of temperance, he begins with abstinence, about which he considers four things. First, the species of abstinence which bears on food, and especially its act of fasting. Second, the vice opposed to it, gluttony. Third, the other species, which is sobriety. Fourth, the vice opposed to it, drunkenness.

As for the first, he shows that abstinence in food is a special virtue from the special matter it must govern, which also has a special difficulty because the use of food is so naturally necessary and its pleasure more intense and thus it is most difficult to restrain. Delight in clothing and the like, by which nature is fostered, is less because nature can be fostered even without expensive clothing. It is insofar as this is done with pomp and haughtiness that modesty governs it. He treats abstinence in **q. 146**. As for its chief act, which is fasting, by which we afflict the body by absence of food in order to moderate concupiscence and free ourselves for the exercise of the virtues, its obligation and manner of observing it according to positive law – he treats all these in **q. 147**.

He treats the vice opposed to abstinence, gluttony, in **q. 148**, showing how it is a capital vice because it concerns something most delightful and which can thus take on the note of an end for the sake of which many other things are desired or not foregone. It is not of its nature a mortal sin because it is not directly opposed to the love of God and neighbor, but it can become a mortal sin because of what is conjoined to it, namely, damage to bodily healthy or contempt for God, insofar as one cultivates a tendency to gluttony and in satisfying it disobeys the precepts of God (**q. 148**).

Third, Saint Thomas takes up the other species of abstinence, sobriety, which moderates the pleasure of intoxicating
drink because such pleasure as such and primarily can take
away the use of reason due to the strength of the drink, which
is the matter of this act; thus it poses a distinct impediment to
reason beyond the pleasures of food and drink simply speaking. This gives rise to a moral distinction and demands a distinct moral virtue which will primarily and as such govern
the delight of drink insofar as it takes away the use of reason.
Sobriety is discussed in q. 149.

Fourth, he treats the vice opposed to sobriety, namely,
drunkenness, in q. 150. Drunkenness is a mortal sin from its
very genus, because through it one is deprived of the use of
reason, not in a natural manner, as in sleep when all activities
are suspended and one does expose himself to the danger of
doing evil, but in a way beyond the natural, taking away the
use of reason and not suspending all external acts but per-
forming them in a bestial manner. This is intrinsically to commit oneself to the danger of sinning and harming gravely,
although out of ignorance of the power of drink or for some
medicinal need one can sometimes be excused.

The second species of temperance after abstinence is
chastity which governs venereal pleasures – chastity governs
these in a common way, but virginity does so more excellently – and modesty governs circumstances and outward signs.
So he treats first of chastity and modesty, which are not distinguished in this way; second, virginity; third, the vice
opposed to chastity and its species.

First, chastity is a virtue distinct from abstinence because
it governs a special matter where there is a distinct morality;
for reason governs the pleasures of food differently from [the
way] it does venereal pleasures, and the one is licit differently from the other. Modesty is not distinguished from chastity
because it governs the external signs and circumstances of sex
concerning which we especially are shamed, but they all pertain to the same libido and are ordered to the same end and
thus are governed by reason in the same manner. He treats
this virtue in q. 151.

Second, virginity, which is the most excellent form of chastity, as magnificence is the most excellent form of liberality. Three kinds of virginity can be distinguished, one natural and another moral, which is subdivided into the morality of a state of life or by some special virtue other than chastity. Natural virginity consists in the integrity of undefiled members. 'Virgin' comes from green (*virens*) which is due to being unsinged by any excess of heat; hence natural virginity implies freshness of flesh, that is, not yet touched by the heat of concupiscence which is the consummation of the greatest pleasure. The state of virginity on the part of its matter presupposes flesh not voluntarily corrupted or burned, and adds the formal note of proposing to preserve oneself from the experience of sex; just as widowed chastity, after having had carnal experience of sex, implies the resolution to keep chaste in every way. But this although from its matter, which is inexperience of all sexual things, implies a greater excellence, yet from the point of view of its formal notion, or resolution, it does not add a distinct virtue beyond common chastity, since that resolution is not in every way firm; accordingly a virgin does not sin if she marries (1 Corinthians 7, 36). She may break her resolution but she does not act against virtue. In order that with respect to resolution virginity should constitute a special virtue beyond common chastity, the resolution must be made specially virtuous with respect to all sexual experience, such that it renders it illicit even with respect to matrimony, something common chastity does not involve. Therefore virginity consecrated to God by a vow, adds not only the circumstance of religion but also, within the matter proper to chastity, there arises a new and special virtue of remaining inexperienced in all sexual matters. It is not unfitting in the species of chastity and dissipation that a district species should arise from the supposition of another virtue as a required condition, just as adultery, on the supposition of injustice, is a special sin of dissipation. Considered in its form, the virtue of virginity is recoverable, although its matter, total inexperience in sexual matters, it is not recoverable once lost. He treats of all this in **q. 152**.

Third, he treats the vice opposed to chastity, which is dissipation, and its species. He shows how dissipation is a mortal sin from its kind, and is a capital sin as well. It is mortal because it consists in a disordered abuse in the emission of seed which by its nature and nature's author is ordered to the generation of a child. Hence if seed is spent either in a manner contrary to its nature, which is ordered to generation, or contrary to the role of educating the child which will be born, since generation is intended by one to whom the education of the child is not entrusted (as in simple fornication, which implies that the parents do not live together, although by their coming together the education of the child naturally devolves upon them). Hence this inordinate abuse in dissipation goes against the charity owed to God and neighbor in a grave matter, namely, the order of nature in the generation of a human being. It is a capital sin because its matter is most pleasurable and consequently most desirable, hence it takes on the note of final cause from which arise many sins, committed or not avoided because of it. He treats this in **q. 153**.

He treats the species of dissipation in **q. 154**. Saint Thomas derives them either from the person being generated, who is the end of the generative act, or from the persons engaged in the act, since from different abuses relative to diverse persons the disorder of dissipation arises. On the part of the person being generated, the abuse of dissipation either completely prevents generation by interposing a physical impediment, or impedes only the fitting upbringing of the child but not generation itself, which is the moral impediment to the child conceived. If it comes about in the first way, it is a sin against nature, and it is called that because physically and naturally it impedes conception in the abuse of seed and thus is opposed even to physical nature. This sin against nature has three species: bestiality, when coitus is had with a living thing of another species; sodomy, in which the partner is of the same species but whose sex is inappropriate; effeminacy which spills seed without access to the other, and this is a mortal sin in its very kind, whether with a man or a woman, because in both cases the seed is intended for generation alone, though the virile seed is principal and active.

If the physical generation of the child is not prevented but only his fitting upbringing, if for example the parents do not bind themselves to live together for the sake of the child's upbringing, although in the human species it is absolutely necessary that the child be reared by both parents, then this is simple fornication. The malice of this sin derives from the fact that it is damaging to the child because those who thus engage in sex naturally establish themselves as parents yet decline to become natural upbringers, not wishing the parental obligation of rearing the child, since they can leave one another at will. Even if someone wished to rear and educate a child thus conceived, since it is not done out of obligation by both parents but out of private will, it does not excuse the act, which of its nature requires both parents and demands that they together rear the child.

If the disorder of dissipation comes about not only on the part of the child conceived but also on the part of the person with whom the act is done, different species of the vice result. If the person is one to whom special reverence is owed, one related by blood, there is incest; or if the person belongs to another as spouse, there is adultery, which is injury to that spouse; if it is a young virgin in the care of another (young women naturally keep their virginity until marriage because virginity is the natural dowry of the woman, distinct from any dowry of fortune) it is ravishment; if it is a person consecrated to God by a vow, it is sacrilege. If violence be added, the young person torn away from her protector, this is rape. All these are discussed in **q. 154**.

3. Potential Parts

Saint Thomas now turns from the subjective to the potential parts of temperance. There are three of them: continence, clemency, and modesty.

Continence can be understood in either of two ways: first, as the restraining of the passions in sexual matters, and then it is the same as chastity. Second, as reason's resistance to the surge of passion, and that is how it is understood here. It is less perfect than temperance and secondary to it because it does not restrain those passions, but keeps reason from being led by vehement passion, and thus the continent person has a less efficacious power of reason than the temperate person because continence does not extend to dominating the appetite which is subject to vehement passions but manages not to be led by them. Thus one cannot at the same time be continent and temperate in act, but only in habit. Because the passions of concupiscence with respect to sex and food are most vehement, continence in their regard is continence simply speaking. He discusses this in **q. 155**.

He treats incontinence, the opposed vice, in the following article. Like its contrary, it pertains to the will because it permits the will to be led by the passions and does not strengthen it against them when they arise. Thus, the incontinent man does not sin from a habit of will, but because of the upsurge of passion against which he makes no resistance. The incontinent person becomes accustomed to sin out of passion but not from habit and malice. Although passion frequently conquers it does not habituate the will to choose, leaving it, however, disposed not to resist passion but to be led by it. A sign of this is that will is not confirmed with respect to the base object, but rather the incontinent person feels penitence once the act is done and passion subsides. In this he is unlike the intemperate person who, because he has a habit of choosing in a depraved way and not just a disposition not to resist. He treats incontinence in **q. 156**.

The second potential part of temperance is mercy – as well as gentleness – whose task it is to refrain from anger about another's wrong, but not in the principal matter of temperance, which is concupiscence. Gentleness and mercy differ because mercy has as its matter the mitigation of punishments, particularly those due to law, but within the limits of justice. It is the virtue of the superior toward the inferior and is especially fitting for the prince. Gentleness governs anger as causative of evil, not legal punishment, and thus properly involves equals. He treats this in **q. 157**.

He treats the vices opposed to these virtues in the two following questions. And first he treats the vice opposed to gentleness, irascibility, which is opposed to gentleness by way of excess. Failure to feel anger even when there is a reasonable cause for doing so, the vice due to defect, has no name. Since revenge is especially desirable, as especially satisfying, it takes on the note of an end for the sake of which many other things are done or omitted. That is why it is a capital vice. It covers many species of sin although the passion of wrath is one species: this is due to the different motives for seeking revenge. For some are called flammable because they are swiftly moved to anger from the prospect of quick revenge; others are called bitter, because they are excessively saddened by injury and filled with bile and for this reason stir up anger; others finally are called difficult, because they perceive vengeance as fulfilling and are thus especially affected by it and find it difficult to remove. Of these he speaks in **q. 158**.

He treats the vice opposed to mercy in the next question. This is cruelty, which makes the soul harsh rather than gentle in mitigating punishment for wrongs. If one is excessively cruel, rejoicing in torture and taking delight in pain, he is called savage or feral, for in this a man becomes like the beasts. He treats this in **q. 159**.

The third potential part of temperance is modesty. While some understand it broadly as moderation in all interior and exterior acts related to the pleasures of touch, and others take it more strictly as the governance of external acts, Thomas takes a middle course and understands modesty as including the moderation of all actions which are aimed at orderliness and maturity, and thus it comprises some interior and some exterior actions. Saint Thomas subdivides it into four species, because there are four things in a man which especially display orderliness and maturity – not with respect to another's evils, but with respect to one's own. First, the desire for excellence, whereby one wants to be considered above others and not keep his own place, and this can destroy order and structure when it is excessive. Second is the vain curiosity concerning knowledge, especially of sensible things, since this dissolves inner order and diverts one from the seriousness of occupations. The third concerns exterior acts whether serious or comic in which man's composition and gravity especially goes glimmering. The fourth has to do with the external outfit and adornment of the person, when luxury dominates and there is a great need of structure and order. Humility is concerned with the first; studiousness with the second; as for the third, ribaldry (*eutrapelia*) is concerned with the comic, good order with the serious; elegance concerns the fourth. So much for the treatment of modesty in general (**q. 160**).

He then takes up the species of modesty in the order given. And first humility, considering first the virtue itself; second the opposed vice; third, especially the pride of the first man and the punishment consequent upon it. With respect to humility itself he gives its proper motive and morality, its power of restraining the desire for disproportionate honor by the consideration of one's own defects, which may also cause one to judge himself unworthy of an honor he really deserves. The reason is that while one can truly judge himself unworthy of the honor he has, given his awareness of his deficiencies, he can still judge himself worthy of them considered as gifts of God lest he be cast down in spirit. Thus the motive of humility arises chiefly from reverence for and subjection to God and other men, estimating oneself according to one's deficiencies, by which one is indeed unworthy. Magnanimity and humility turn on the same thing, accordingly, that is, proportionate honors, but out of different motives: magnanimity as seeks and impels to great honors but proportionate ones because of the gifts of God and one's own achievements, and secondarily represses disproportionate honors, not, however, out of a sense of one's own deficiency, as humility does, but by comparison of disproportionate to proportionate honor. Humility, however, as it were by the lowering due to the awareness of one's deficiencies, causes one to think himself unworthy of any honor in the light of those deficiencies. It retains, however, the honor proportionate to oneself, not dejecting the spirit beyond what is fitting with respect to God's gifts. Thus it proceeds by refraining and introducing a modification into movements that tend immoderately to excellence. And because the matter of this refraining is not the pleasure of touch, which is the principal matter of temperance, but one's own excellence, humility is a potential part of temperance. As for the motive from which it proceeds, namely divine reverence, with respect to which it recognizes its own defects, it is more excellent than the other moral virtues. Thanks to it a man is especially advanced, namely, subjecting himself completely to right order, because he does not think himself excellent by any measure. He treats humility in **q. 161**.

Second, he considers the opposite vice, which by way of excess is pride or by way of defect, when one becomes completely cast down, considering his own vileness in an unfitting way and without reference to the gifts of God. Pride is directly opposed to humility, with respect to motive, with respect to the matter with which it deals, and with respect to the object it desires. In motive, because humility out of divine reverence subjects itself and thinks itself unworthy of any honor because of its deficiencies; pride, however, excuses itself from divine reverence, either positively, directly contemning God, which is the worst kind of pride, or only privatively, when one so pursues his own excellence that he takes himself away from God, not giving him reverence and honor, but arrogating them to himself. In matter, because humility looks to one's own deficiencies, whereas pride aspires "after great things or matters above me" (Psalm 133, 1). In object, because humility looks to its own lowering due to one's deficiencies, but pride to its own exaltation, not in this or that matter, but in everything. Thus, though materially, with respect to remote matter, pride seems generally to be included in every sin, insofar as in it is found some contempt of God, by turning oneself away from his rule and law, formally pride is a special sin because of its motive, since it intends one's proper excellence in every matter, and therefore it is a capital vice, excellence being most desirable, and thus capable of taking on the note of an end for the sake of which many things can be desired or not avoided. Its subject is will because it does look solely to corporeal excellence but also to spiritual excellence and universally in whatever matter; that is why it must belong to will which is a spiritual and universal faculty, and has the power of tending toward arduous things by hope and boldness. He treats pride in **q. 162**.

Because the sin of the first man calls for a special consideration of pride as to its gravity, Saint Thomas treats it here. For the first man wanted to be like God, not in a likeness of nature, but of knowledge, as the angel wanted to be like him in power. The angel is by nature full of knowledge, whereas man had infused knowledge by a gratuitous gift, not because of his nature. Therefore the angel wanted to be like God, not in knowledge, but in majesty and power, seeking to "sit on the mountain of the covenant" (Isaiah 14, 13), wanting to be singularly and independently great. But man wanted to be like God in the fullness of knowledge, wanting to know good and evil like gods, without subjection to and rule by God. He treats of pride and the gravity of this sin in **q. 163**. Of the effects of this sin, that is, the penalties following on it, such as death, exclusion from paradise, and the like, he treats in **q. 164**. He treats the cause of this sin, namely, temptation, and the manner and order in which it was done, in **q. 165**.

The second species of modesty is studiousness, which restrains the excessive desire for knowledge, that is, curiosity. Studiousness does not bear on knowledge itself, but on the application to knowing, because application is an act of will which is called use; therefore studiousness is in the will, both because of the act it restrains and because of the amplitude of the matter on which it turns, that is, applying oneself to know both intellectually and by the senses. And because it moderates the desire or application of knowing, it is a moral virtue. He treats it in **q. 166**.

Of the opposite vice, which is curiosity, he treats next, in **q. 167**. It implies inordinate excess in the application of the will to know, hence the matter of this vice must be understood most formally, as the inordinate application to knowledge as knowledge. For the indulgent and gluttonous desire the inordinate use of touch by which we sense and know, not, however, to know but in order to take pleasure. But the curious person seeks sensibles even if they harm him, because he seeks only knowledge of them. This distinguishes the delight of curiosity from libidinous pleasure, since the latter arises from the use of touchables in order that they might cause pleasure, the former precisely in order to know.

The third species of modesty is concerned with actions and external doings, whether serious or comic, with which ribaldry and good order are concerned, not under the note of obligation and honorableness, as are affability and truth, which are parts of justice, but according to moderation so that one neither exceeds nor falls short in the things he does, according to composure and external decency, even in recreation. Of these virtues and the superfluity and defect in play, he treats in **q. 168**.

The fourth species of modesty has to do with external adornment in clothes and retinue. Of it and its opposed vices, especially the excess of women in dress and make-up, he treats in **q. 169**.

c. The Precepts of Temperance

Finally, he treats of the precepts of temperance, especially concerning sexual matters, and the precepts of the other virtues joined to temperance (**q. 170**).

2. On Special States of Life

Having explained all the virtues and vices, which apply generally to all men, he finally discusses things special to the states or conditions of men. The theologian does not consider states of the political order, but only of the ecclesiastical and Christian order, which come from the Holy Spirit distributing things as he wills. The Apostle reduces conditions and ministries to three types, saying, "Now there are varieties of gifts, but the same Spirit; and there are varieties of ministries, but the same Lord, and there are varieties of workings, but the same God, who works all things in all." (1 Corinthians 12, 4–6) By varieties of gifts he can be taken to mean graces gratuitously given (*gratia gratis data*), which are not common to all, but distributed to some. Grace gratuitously given is in turn divided into four kinds, for some belong to knowledge, as with prophecy and discernment of spirits, etc., some pertain to speech, as the word of wisdom, of knowledge, the gift of tongues, etc., and some pertain to activity, as the grace of healing and grace of the virtues. Sanctifying grace and charity rather than grace gratuitously given belong to will, rectifying it with respect to the ultimate end.

By the varieties of deeds Saint Thomas understands different modes of life, such as the active and contemplative lives, which are called different because they exercise difference actions and operations.

By varieties of ministries he understands different states, offices and ministries in the Church, such as the state of the bishop, the religious, and so forth. For from all these the mystical body of the Church is composed.

a. Grace Gratuitously Given

He begins first with the divisions of graces, or of graces gratuitously given, in which, according to the three kinds mentioned, he deals first with those that pertain to knowledge and need a special light which is comprised under the prophetic light.

With respect to prophecy, he considers first what pertains to prophecy as such, then what belongs to some special perfection of prophecy which is called rapture. There are four things to take up concerning prophecy itself: first, the essence of prophecy; second, its cause; third, the means or species through which it comes about; fourth, its kinds.

He considers the essence of prophecy both on the part of its genus, which is knowledge, and its difference, which pertains to divine revelation making something known in transitory manner. From the point of view of its material object it extends to everything subject to the divine light, especially having to do with the future or the far off. Prophecy belongs to knowledge formally, although dispositively it can pertain to will. Prophecy involves a twofold action on the part of God and a twofold way of being acted upon on our side. One is, as it were, antecedently disposing, namely, the motion of will by which the intention of a man is elevated to perceive divine things, and Job speaks of it in this way, "The inspiration of the Almighty giveth understanding." (Job 33, 8) The other is revelation which illumines the mind so it can perceive what God reveals to it; and prophecy is completed there because the obscurity of ignorance is then formally removed, "He discovereth deep things out of darkness." (John 12, 22) His light is not given to the intellect of the prophet in the manner of a habit, but as a transient light, which is given in dependence on actual inspiration and revelation because prophecy is ordered to knowing supernatural things and things hidden from us without knowing their principles, because the prophet does not see the divine essence in which all objects are contained, nor can it extend to the vision of it as do our theology and infused science: prophecy would be voided if the divine essence were seen, for prophecy sees things in a similitude and darkness and from a distance, whereas in the divine essence all things are seen in full light. That is why a prophet cannot infer the knowledge of his object from principles had permanently and habitually as such; he must depend on an illumination or manifestation made at the time by another who sees those causes, and that is God. Faith is infused in the manner of a habit because it is not given in order to see something from the power of its cause or of an illumination but to assent to the testimony of the one speaking. It is not then a purely intellectual light which has its root in any manifestation of its principles, but a light of intellect, as moved by will, in which it has its principle. He speaks of the essence of prophecy in **q. 171**.

Second, he considers the efficient cause of prophecy. With respect to supernatural prophecy and the infusion of the prophetic light, the immediate cause is God, although with respect to the proposal of objects and the disposition and coordination of images, both in the imagination and in intellect, angels can be intermediate causes of prophecy, just as one angel can enlighten another. Natural prophecy, by which future events are known either in their natural causes or under the influence of a demon, does not have God for its immediate cause (**q. 172**).

Third, he treats the means by which the prophetic light attains its objects. The means are created images or likenesses by which the things involved in the prophecy are represented.

These are sometimes infused *de novo* by God but are sometimes acquired by the senses and are coordinated in a new and higher way as required for a judgment of these things: the act of prophecy is completed in that judgment. No alienation of the senses is required, particularly of the inner senses, but prophecy ordinarily comes about with a return to sense images. He discusses this in **q. 173**.

Fourth, he discusses the kinds of prophecy. Prophecy can be divided either from the point of view of its essential definition, on the part of its material object, or on the part of the means by which the thing to be prophesied about is represented, insofar as the likenesses are more or less abstract and express – this last is both accidental and twofold.

In the first way, prophecy is of one atomic species and is not further subdivided because the formal notion is the same, namely, divine revelation revealing outside the Word, and just as the light of the revelation of faith is of one species only: that is why the Holy Doctor said above (q. 171, a. 3, ad 3) that it has a formally specific unity.

In the second way prophecy is divided into prophecy of prescience and prophecy of warning, for prescience concerns things as they ought to be done absolutely, but warning according to certain conditions as the effect is brought about by lower causes.

In the third way three kinds of prophecy are distinguished, two extremes which are not properly covered by the definition of prophecy, by exceeding or falling short of it. And there is another midway between them, which is prophecy proper. The lowest and imperfect extreme is when someone acts by the instinct or inspiration of God but does not receive supernatural light, as when Samson was moved to cut down the Philistines. The other extreme, by way of excess, is when someone receives a light so perfect that he has a purely intellectual vision of supernatural truths without any images, almost the vision of the divine essence which perhaps occurs in rapture. This belongs to the most excellent prophets, as is said in 2 Kings 23, 3–4: "The strong one of Israel spoke, the ruler of men, the just ruler, the fear of God. As the light of the morning when the sun riseth, shineth in the morning without clouds . . ." By the light is meant clarity, not as of the sun, which would be a vision of the divine essence, but lower than that, like the light of dawn, which exceeds the night and the obscurity of faith, while with reference to what is seen there is removal of clouds, that is of bodily images. In the middle kind of prophecy something is revealed with bodily and imaginary vision, for this presents an intelligible truth behind a veil or in obscurity, like a light between clouds. "And we have the word of prophecy, surer still, to which you do well to attend, as to a lamp shining in a dark place, until the day dawns and the morning star rises in your hearts." (2 Peter 1, 19) Here the darkness of prophecy is not located in the light or lamp but on the side of the thing seen or the means, "shining in a dark place," as in the clouds. There are degrees in this kind of prophecy because sometimes something is revealed with an external bodily sign, like the boiling caldron and rod of Jeremiah 1, 11–13. Sometimes something is heard or seen in imaginary vision alone, and the more expressly the higher the degree, and if someone sees while awake, this is more perfect than while sleeping, and if while awake one sees a person speaking to him, whether in the likeness of an angel or of God, these are signs that one is nearer to the source of prophecy. Of these divisions of prophecy and the fact that none of them pertains to the blessed who see all things immediately in God, he speaks in **q. 174.**

After prophecy he takes up rapture which does not involve a light distinct from the prophetic but a special mode, namely, by the elevation of knowledge above its connatural manner, which involves reference to the senses. Rapture implies a mode exceeding the connatural way of knowing and thus comes about with some violence, taking the intellect out of its connatural mode, but this violence does not refer to will when it is borne in ecstasy toward the beloved since that comes about through love and voluntary inclination (**q. 175**).

The second grace gratuitously given is the gift of tongues, which in substance is natural, that is, to know different languages, but can be supernatural in its mode either because it is infused by God and not acquired, as can happen when other natural knowledge is infused, or because in speaking one's own language it comes about divinely that one is understood by men of another language. This is more fitting in the first way when one can understand others speaking their own languages. He treats this in **q. 176.**

The third grace gratuitously given is the grace of speech, that is, that someone is effective in persuasion both with respect to instructing the mind of the hearer and to moving his affections such that he freely hears and loves what is proposed. No new knowing habit need be added for this, but only that a man be moved by God when he speaks so that he presents well and is heard well and thus persuades. He discusses this in **q. 177.**

The fourth grace gratuitously given is the grace of miracles, also called the acts of the powers: it includes the grace of healing because it even heals miraculously. A man is not given a habitual power to work miracles, because no created power can act above the common course of nature changing things themselves as a principal cause and when he wants, but God uses him as an instrument by some interior or exterior act of man bringing about such changes, for the confirmation of faith and the utility of the Church (**q. 178**).

b. Divisions of Activities

After the divisions of graces gratuitously given, there follows a division of the activities by which men live, and these are generally reduced to two kinds of life, the active and contemplative, since man's life is properly accorded to reason, and reason is adequately divided by active and contemplative (**q. 179**). He treats of these two lives generally at first, establishing their difference, then takes them up singly; and finally, he compares them to one another.

He treats especially of the contemplative life, considering its essence, object, act and antecedent, and concomitant dispositions. The essential note of the contemplative is that it aims solely at knowledge of the truth. The chief truth it can aim at is knowledge of the ultimate end, which is divine truth. And because the appetitive power aims or intends and thereby moves the other powers, even intellect, the motive of the contemplative life is in will though it is formally in intellect. In the will, with respect to antecedent dispositions, are the moral virtues by which the appetitive part is perfected, lest the reason of the one contemplating be disturbed by passions. Thus in order that one be moved to contemplation it is presupposed that the will is rectified and stilled by moral virtues. On the side of the intellectual power by which contemplation is formally exercised there are a number of concurrent acts, for we contemplate some truths that are inferred from principles made manifest to us, so that acceptance of principles is presupposed, and then inference or manifestation from these of the truth to be contemplated. Finally, fixed knowledge of the inferred truth, and that is contemplation. On the side of the objects, although it is principally concerned with divine truth, still it arrives at it by way of created effects as by antecedent dispositions, nor can it come to the vision of God except in the other life (**q. 180**).

Second, he considers the active life which is essentially ordered to operation, and therefore the moral virtues by which we are directed in virtuous operations pertain to it not only dispositively but essentially, since it is exercised in them (**q. 181**).

As for the comparison of the two lives, the active and contemplative, he asks which is more worthy and which of greater merit given its kind, and whether they are impediments to one another, in **q. 182**.

c. Divisions of Ministries

After the divisions of graces and activities, he goes on to discuss what pertains to the division of ministries according to various offices and states which serve the Church. He takes up two things. First, the very notion of state and office, in general, and then, two, in particular.

First, Saint Thomas distinguishes a threefold diversity among members of the Church or of the faithful. One is ordered to perfection, another is ordered to action, a third is ordered to the beauty and ordered disposition of the Church.

The diverse states are ordered to perfection, from beginners to the proficient. By "state" is meant a disposition implying immobility and rest, because one "stands" when he comes to rest. In moral matters, immobility comes about according to some obligation, especially stemming from a vow or contract, and thus the notion of state derives from obligation, as in the state of matrimony, the religious state, that of bishops, etc. Secondarily and imperfectly beginners and the proficient are said to be states.

Different offices in the Church are ordered to the performance of diverse actions, because as is said in Romans 12, 4, "For just as in one body we have many members, yet all the members have not the same function . . ." Thus we have the office of deacon, subdeacon, and so on.

The different grades – in the offices and states there are lower and higher grades – bring about the beauty which arises from the distinction and disposition of orders in the Church. He discusses this in **q. 183**.

Saint Thomas does not go into detail on the diversity of offices and grades which pertain to sacred ministry because they are treated in the sacrament of Orders. Of the states, he omits matrimony, which pertains to the sacrament of matrimony, which was to be discussed later. Hence he treats only the state of the perfect, for the state of beginners and proficients are reduced to that of the perfect as, generally speaking, the imperfect is to the perfect.

The state of perfection is considered by Saint Thomas in two ways. First, in general, second with special reference to the episcopal and religious states. He considers the state of perfection in general as subsumed under charity which, as the Apostle says, is the bond of perfection because it unites us to God in whom our supreme perfection consists. Charity can be perfected in two ways. In one way, by the total exclusion of its contrary, namely, mortal sin: the perfection of charity cannot be had in a state of mortal sin. In another way, by the exclusion of those things which impede or retard the excellence of charity, whether with respect to God or neighbor. The greater excellence of charity is in the greater reception of the love of God and in beneficence toward neighbor. The counsels order us to this since they dispose us to give ourselves to the love of God. And since a state implies some obligation for one to hold unchangingly to something, it is not the same thing to be perfect and to have the state of perfection, since the state involves an obligation to perfection, but not everyone who obliges himself to something immediately has it. Wherefore the state of perfection implies an obligation to the things which pertain to perfection in charity and the Christian life. This obligation arises in a twofold manner, since one can either oblige himself to the things by which he acquires perfection or do the things by which he communicates it to others. The first is, as it were, a passive state of the perfect, and this is the state of religious. The second is the state of the perfect, as it were, actively, as with prelates who must feed and teach, which is to communicate perfection. Not just any prelate has this state, but only those bound by perpetual obligation to feed others, even giving their life for their sheep, which is the most excellent act of charity. Such are the bishops. Hence there is a fitting transition from the first order of the state of perfection to the second, that is, that bishops be selected from those in the religious state, if they are indeed religious (**q. 184**).

He treats specially of the state of bishops, which is more perfect. How may it be desired? The work may be desired, but not the dignity. Hence the Apostle did not sa, those who desire the episcopacy desire the good of being set above, but the good work – "If anyone is eager for the office of bishop, he desires a good work." 1 Timothy 3, 1 – speaking quite formally, as if to say, the great work is desired as work. Similarly, on how it can be refused or resigned because of peril, and the like, he treats in **q. 185.**

Second, he treats in particular the state of perfection of religious. He does four things. First, he asks in what this state consists. Second, what actions licitly belong to religious. Third, the kinds of religious. Fourth, on going into religious life.

First, the religious state implies giving oneself over and an obligation to serve God, tending to the perfection of charity by excluding the things that can impede it. There are three things which especially turn men from God and impede him:

external goods which are possessed; the good of one's own body, which is fulfilled by sense pleasures, among which the sexual looms largest; finally, the good of one's own will. Therefore the state of perfection for religious ought to cut off these three. First, by the vow of poverty, the second by the vow of chastity, the third by the vow of obedience. And they should be fixed by vow and have perpetual stability as is required by the notion of state. To these three are reduced "all that is in the world," namely, "the lust of the flesh" which chastity counters; "the lust of the eyes" which pertains to the possession of riches, against which poverty is set; and "the pride of life" which is the free puffing up of the spirit, against which is set obedient subjection. (1 John 2, 16) He discusses this in **q. 186.**

With regard to the second, he excludes what some have said are illicit actions of religious, namely, teaching, preaching, engaging in secular business when charity requires, begging and living by alms, and other like actions which are ordered to the end of charity and are not against the rule. He shows these are licit for religious in **q. 187.**

With regard to the third, namely, the distinction and variety of religious, he shows that all religious agree in one common end, namely, that they tend to the perfection of charity, but they differ in means or the particular ends which each intends in order to attain differently the one common end. Or in one order they can perform different exercises from in another, with greater or lesser rigor or austerity, and so on. An order can aim at whatever the perfection of charity toward God and neighbor includes, and be set up according to different works, for example, of the contemplative life, such as praying, study, chanting the psalms, or the works of the active life, teaching, preaching, redeeming, curing the sick, or even to both kinds of work at once, including the active and contemplative. He discusses this in **q. 188.**

Regarding the fourth, namely, entry into religious life, he show, who is ready for entry, how one can be fittingly bound to it by a vow, how the young can be inducted and admitted, how one may change orders, and other like things pertaining to entry (**q. 189**).

Detailed Outline of Third Part

The Third Part

The Order and Connections of Its Treatises

Christ

After Saint Thomas treats God as he is in himself and as he is the cause of creatures, and especially the end of the rational creature who can attain him through his acts, there remains to consider God as the way by which we return to him through the redemption of sins. That is, he now treats of God the savior from the fullness of whose grace we receive everything and from which we derive all the efficacy and power of our reparation. Saint Thomas divides the treatise on God the Savior into three principal parts. First, he considers the mystery of the Incarnation itself and the perfections belonging to Christ, his actions and his life. This extends through **q. 59**. Second, he turns to the means that unite us to him and by which reparation is applied to us, namely, the sacraments. Third, the effect and end to which we come through this reparation, namely, immortal glory.

1, The Savior Himself
a. The Mystery of the Incarnation
In order to explain the mystery of the Incarnation, St. Thomas first discusses the question *whether it is (an est)*, namely, the fittingness of the Incarnation on the part of God, the principal cause and motive was his immense goodness: "Because of the loving kindness of our God, wherewith the Orient from on high has visited us." (Luke 1, 78) On our side, the principal

motive was our salvation, for the sake of which he came down from heaven and was made man. Saint Thomas discusses the fittingness of the Incarnation from the side of God, which is that he might communicate himself to the creature in the fullest manner, and its necessity on our part – not absolute necessity, but in order that an end might be achieved, namely, severe satisfaction for sin and full redemption. From this as a principle he also infers that, if this redemption were the motive for the sake of which the Incarnation was decreed, were this motive to fail, another decree would have been given such that it would have come about in another way or absolutely would not have come about (**q. 1**).

1. On the Hypostatic Union

Having considered the question *an est*, Saint Thomas goes on to explain the notion and essence of this mystery. The whole essence of the Incarnation consists in the union of two natures, divine and human, in the one Person of the Word. Knowledge of it requires, accordingly, a grasp of this union and an understanding of the two extremes. He first discusses the union, and second the extremes united.

With respect to the union, he considers its notion by showing it to be completely different from anything known by the philosophers who were the guides of heretics. For the philosophers never knew a substantial union which would involve a *supposit* [or individual] and not just constitute a nature, for here natures remain together and mixed in the same person. Heretics, unable to understand this, fell into two opposed errors. For some, such as Eutyches and Dioscurus, wishing to safeguard the substantial nature of the union, said there was a union in nature, such that from the divine and human nature one nature would result, rather than that both would remain in the same person. Thus they introduced change, or even violence, into the divine nature. Others like Nestorius went to the other extreme, seeking to safeguard at all costs the distinction and mingling of natures, denied that there was a substantial union and affirmed only an accidental one, holding that each nature was a distinct person. But this is to deny a substantial union. Others more closely approximating the Catholic truth said that Christ's person is one but with two supposits, for they thought that the Word assumed an individual man, and assumed this to his person, that is, to his dignity, distinguishing between person and supposit. Finally others, in order to correct this, said that he assumed not an integral or individual man, but body separately, then soul separately, which are accidentally united to the Word.

But the Catholic faith explains this union thus, that the divine person or supposit (they are the same) assumes unto himself not some individual man but human nature, composed of body and soul united in the notion of the nature but not subsisting of itself, prevented from having its own personality because its supposit is the divine person. Thus he communicates to it his own supposit, not as accidentally sustaining or by denomination, but as making it substantially terminated or subsisting. From such a union this person is made doubly subsisting, that is, in two natures, and therefore in the notion and office of subsisting it is composite, not simple, that is, not subsisting in one nature alone. Of this union and what it posits or changes on the side of humanity and how it is the highest union in that in which it is, namely in the person (for in the Trinity the Persons are not united but are one), and also how it is said to be done through grace and what merits it involves he treats in **q. 2.**

2. The Extremes United
Having explained the union, he turns to the extremes united. One extreme is something which assumes, namely the Word, and the other the assumed, namely, human nature, with which other perfections are assumed, such as grace and knowledge, and other imperfections in the nature assumed are lost.

a. The Assuming Extreme
First then of the extreme that assumes, which is the person to whom what is assumed comes, through the mediation of omnipotence as the power effecting the assumption. Therefore omnipotence or nature is said to be the principle *by which* (*quo*) of the assuming. The Person assuming is understood to

terminate the nature assumed by reason of the relative pro-
priety which is the divine personality. Because the divine relations share the same power, all the Persons can assume the
same nature and one Person several natures, because of the
infinite eminence involved in the terminating (**q. 3**).

b. The Extreme Assumed
Then he discusses the extreme assumed in which he first considers the nature assumed, then the perfections assumed with
it, and finally imperfections. With respect to the nature itself,
he first considers it as a complete thing assumed. Second, the
parts of this nature which are also assumed. Third, the order
followed in assuming the parts.

As for the nature itself, he shows that what is assumed is
human nature in the singular, for he does not assume man or
person as if there were in Christ two persons, and thus the
union does not come about substantially (**q. 4**).

As for the parts of human nature, which are body and
soul as constituting the nature, he shows their unity to be
from the Word, and this against those heretics who erred with
respect to the body and the soul of Christ. Some denied
Christ's was a true body but only imaginary, namely, the
Manicheans. Some said that it was a true body, but celestial
and not corruptible, not of flesh and blood. Hence he shows
that the Word assumed a true body with flesh and blood and
all the parts truly belonging to human nature. With regard to
the soul, some heretics denied that he assumed a soul, but
that the Word serves as soul, namely, Arius and Apollinaris,
which would take away true human nature. Others said that
he had a soul, but not a mind, the Word serving as mind, as
some of the followers of Apollinaris said. He argues against
these in **q. 5**.

As for the order followed in assuming the parts, since
order involves prior and posterior, he distinguishes the priority of time and the priority of nature. Priority of time is wholly excluded, because the Word assumes the whole of human
nature at once along with all its parts. The priority of nature
or causality is taken either on the part of the thing assumed or
on the part of the agent, that is, the one assuming. On the side

of the assumed, one part is found to be prior to another, for example, soul is prior to body both in dignity and in causality. For the flesh is informed and made animate and thus human. Thus on the side of the assumed, the body is assumed by means of soul, as a mediator of more worth and making worthy by constituting the flesh; just as the Word assumed the soul by the medium of spirit, because it is thanks to spirit that it is in the image of God, which fits the purpose of the assumption, namely, to reform the image of God in man. On the side of the agent, the order of nature follows both on intention and execution. In the order of intention, the Word first assumed the whole nature, then its parts, because that which is whole and entire is first and chiefly intended, rather than that which is incomplete and imperfect, as parts are. In the order of execution it is the reverse, because execution begins with the imperfect and is consummated and completed by the perfect, and thus assumption begins with the parts. Of all this he treats in **q. 6.**

c. Perfections Assumed along with Humanity

Having examined one term, what was assumed, its nature and constitutive parts, he goes on to consider the perfections assumed along with humanity, which chiefly attach to the part of the soul capable of these perfections.

He considers three of the greatest perfections in the soul of Christ, namely, grace, which perfected his soul and will; knowledge, which perfected his intellect; and power, which enabled him to act excellently.

With respect to grace, Saint Thomas considers its excellence, first insofar as it is a personal grace, and places special perfections in the soul of Christ. Second, the grace of being a source or head, able to give grace to others out of his fullness. With reference to the first, he shows that there was habitual grace in Christ, which conferred an additional sanctity over and above the personal sanctity by which his soul, thanks to its union with the Person of the Word, not only participates in an accidental way in the divine nature, but is also immediately joined with it in a person and is made a consort of the divine nature by the mediation of personality and is not only a quality.

Beyond this he had habitual grace with every excellence of the virtues and gifts which do not involve some imperfection of condition, such as faith and hope. Thus it can be said that there was fullness of grace in him because every effect of grace which signifies perfection was in him. And finally, an infinity of grace, which can be threefold: in the substance of grace, according to its quantity, and according to relation. The infinity in the substance of grace is not an absolute infinity in every genus (for only God is thus infinite), but in a determinate genus, namely of grace, and thus the form in general and the substance of such a form is called finite, since it has every perfection pertaining to its genus; thus infinity and fullness are the same. Infinity of quantity, that is, according to an intensive increase, also belongs to grace in Christ: because it is the highest, at least in ordinary power (*potentia*) which that species of grace naturally demands, although *de potentia absoluta* it can increase and is not infinite. Infinity according to relation is infinity of moral dignity, which the grace of Christ has from union with the divine Person and with respect to him: in this way too it is infinite. With this grace, considered personally, **q. 7** deals.

In **q. 8** he treats the grace of Christ insofar as he is the 'head' of grace. Three conditions are present in the grace of Christ which pertain to the notion of head and with reference to which he is metaphorically called the head. For head signifies principle or primacy, perfection, and influx or direction. He is called head in the sense of principle and primacy because he is closest to God. He is called head in the sense of perfection because in him there is the fullness of grace, as the fullness of sensation is in the head. He is called head because of inflowing because we all receive grace from him. The angels too, whom he precedes in grace and fullness, receive from him many effects of grace, although not in the manner of redemption..

The second perfection assumed along with humanity by the Son of God is knowledge. In him are all the treasures of the wisdom and knowledge of God. He treats this knowledge first in general, then specifically. There is in Christ not only the divine knowledge which belongs to him insofar as he is God, but a created knowledge as well which belongs to him as man, and this is threefold. There is in him the beatifying knowledge of the vision of God. There is an infused knowledge by which he knows outside the Word both natural and supernatural things in the way the angels do. Finally there is natural knowledge insofar as in the human manner he draws knowledge from the senses and from images in the way any man does. This common treatment of his knowledge is found in q. 9.

He goes on to discuss these kinds of knowledge in particular. First, the beatifying science through which the soul of Christ intuitively sees God, though not comprehensively, but he grasps all the things that God does by the science of vision because all created things are subject to him and he must judge them all as he sees them all in God (q. 10).

The second kind of knowledge or science is as such infused. He considers the objects to which it extends, its mode, and its definition. Its objects are whatever is covered by divine revelation and the natural light outside the vision of the divine essence which constitutes the beatifying vision. The mode of this knowledge is studied under three headings. First, it is not necessarily dependent on phantasms any more than the knowledge of angels is. Second, it is not the result of discourse, although it can employ it in the manner of the rational soul. Third, it was a habitual knowledge, that is, distinguished by different habits, because it had less universal intelligible species than the angels and the foundation of diverse knowability (q. 11).

The third knowledge is acquired and through it Christ knew everything that can be known by the light of the agent intellect from the senses. Nor was this knowledge infused incidentally (per accidens), but was acquired in the connatural manner, on the supposition that he had the other kinds of knowledge: this acquisition on his part does not presuppose a prior ignorance, for he did not learn anything from men or angels or from objects, though by the ministry of angels he was able to use it in order to present to himself certain objects. (q. 12).

The last perfection the soul of Christ assumed is power. Not that the divine omnipotence was communicated to him, but that he has a twofold power: as principal cause and as instrumental cause. As principal cause he has the power of governing his own body and its acts and of illumining through the fullness of grace and knowledge all rational creatures. As instrumental, he has the power to bring about miraculous changes which can be ordered to the mystery of the Incarnation, but not the power to create or annihilate. Power is treated in **q. 13**.

Having enumerated the perfections assumed along with human nature, he considers the defects or imperfections that he sustains and assumes. They are of two kinds, some on the part of the body, some on the part of the soul. On the part of the body, he takes on the defects which accompany a body that can be acted upon: "Surely he hath borne our infirmities and carried our sorrows." (Isaiah 53, 4) On the supposition that he assumed a body that could be acted upon, he took on the necessity of being subject to these things because of nature, not by any necessity contracted by sin: he took them on absolutely voluntarily in taking of such a body. Saint Thomas treats these bodily defects in **q. 14**.

As for the defects on the part of the soul, they are treated in **q. 15**. They can be considered either on the side of intellect, with respect to ignorance, and on the side of will, with respect to sin, or on the part of the sense appetite, with respect to regulated passions, or on the side of excesses (*exorbitantes*) due to the prudence of the flesh. Because of the fullness of habitual and personal grace the soul of Christ excludes whatever is due to actual or habitual sin or to the prudence of the flesh. His fullness of knowledge excludes anything pertaining to privative ignorance. The passions in Christ were regulated even though they imply some painful aspects, such as sadness, sorrow, fear, wrath, and the like, but these are perfectly subject to reason.

d. The Consequences of Union

Having explained the mystery of the Incarnation with respect to union and to the extremes assumed, and the perfections and defects of human nature, there follows in the order of doctrine the treatment of the things consequent on this union and mystery which are attributed to Christ.

Since this mystery consists in the communing of two natures in the unity of one supposit, three things follow on it. Some pertain to the union, insofar as the predicates proper to one nature are said of the other concretely because of the supposit. Some pertain to the unity in existence itself and in person. Others pertain to plurality in acting, because the natures which are the principles of operation remained unconfused.

He treats of the sharing of properties (*idiomatum*) in **q. 16**, showing that all the predicates which are said of the supposit by reason of nature can be predicated of both natures taken concretely, because to be taken concretely is to be taken for the supposit, and thus is verified the truth that God has died and suffered, etc., and that man is creator and God. But if the nature is taken abstractly, such sharing does not take place, because they are not taken for the supposit, but for the nature, and this remains unconfused. Thus it is false to say that divinity has died or that humanity creates, and so on. Similarly if some naming (*appellatio*), precision (*praecisio*), or application (*applicatio*) intervenes which would impede this sharing, as when it is said that this man is placed in a category, but God is not. However if some predicate does not belong to the supposit by reason of nature alone, but by reason of the supposit as well, and implies some repugnance to the supposit, it is not said of it absolutely, but only with a reduplication of the nature, as it is not said that "Christ is a creature," save insofar as he is man, because to be created is something so transcendent that he can also be said of the supposit by reason of itself.

As for the things consequent on the unity of the supposit or person in Christ, he shows that in Christ there is only one substantial existence because this pertains directly to the supposit, which exists absolutely as *what (quod)* [exists]; the natures and parts only coexist as that *whereby (quo)*. Similarly, thanks to the unity of the supposit, numerical unity does not multiply in Christ, and thus he is said to be absolutely one, not two (**q. 17**).

As for what follows on the plurality of natures with respect to powers and acts, he says two things. First, there were in Christ two wills, a human and the divine, and so there were many acts. Many heretics denied the plurality of wills either because they denied that Christ had a soul (Apollinaris), or because they held that he had but one nature made up of the human and divine (Eutyches), or because, though they confessed two distinct natures, they said the human was an instrument of the divine and thus willing and acting do not pertain to the human, but only to be acted upon and moved, and thus only in the divine nature was their will (Sergius and Macarius). But the Catholic faith confesses that there are two wills in Christ, one divine, the other human, and so with all the powers pertaining to human nature. There is no conflict between these wills, but rather the highest agreement (he treats of this in **q. 18**). That he also had two kinds of operation, human and divine, and how through human activity he merited for himself and us, is treated in **q. 19**.

Having explained the things consequent on the union of the Incarnation with reference to Christ himself, he next treats them with respect to the Father. There are some which Christ presents to the Father, and others that the Father presents to Christ.

Christ presents to the Father, first, subjection (**q. 20**). Second, prayer, as our advocate, but he also prays for himself and he was always heard in that he efficaciously asked (of this he treats in **q. 21**). Third, he presents to the Father the ministry of priest, offering himself as a sacrifice for the destruction of sin. Of priesthood and its effect which is eternal by reason of the glory to which it leads, he treats in **q. 22**.

The things the Father presents to Christ come down to two. First, he gives him a sonship, not adoptive but natural, though temporally communicated in the Incarnation. He treats of adoption in **q. 23**. Second, the Father gives predestination to Christ, both passive, namely that this man might be predestined to be the natural son of God in the same supposit [individual], such that there is only a distinction of reason between the subject of predestination, namely that person as man, from the term to which, namely to natural sonship as freely communicated – and active, such that Christ is the cause of our predestination on the part of all its effects. Saint Thomas speaks of the predestination of Christ in **q. 24**.

Finally Saint Thomas considers the things consequent on the union of Incarnation with respect to us, and these come down to two, namely, what we should give to Christ and what he gives to us. We are held to show all subjection and reverence, adoring the person endowed with humanity with the adoration of *latriae*. Hence in the Fourth Synod he was declared anathema who did not adore with one adoration the incarnate God. This adoration is also shown to the cross and image of Christ, with reference to Christ and not absolutely with reference to themselves. *Hyperdulia* is given his Mother and to her sacred humanity considered precisely because of the fullness of grace; *dulia* is offered holy relics. Of adoration he treats in **q. 25**.

The things Christ offers us are included in the office of mediator which follows on the Incarnation; by it Christ reconciles us with God and gives us the gifts of grace. Of the mediator he treats in **q. 26**.

b. On the Life and Deeds of Christ
Up to this point, Saint Thomas has explained the nature of the mystery of the Incarnation, the extremes united, and the things which follow on this union, speaking of them as such and, as it were, in general. Now he gets down to the particular, explaining the mode, and what execution this ineffable union demands, and how God brought its work to life in the middle of the years and brought salvation to the middle of the earth. Thus he treats the things Christ did in this life. Saint Thomas divides this meditation or consideration into four principal parts. First, he considers the entry of the Son of God into this world, being born of the Virgin. Second, the progress of his life in this world. Third, his departure from this world. Fourth, his exaltation above the world.

First, Saint Thomas meditates on Christ's entry by means of his conception to his baptism; for then the unfolding of his life began to be known by men. So he treats his conception, birth, his manifestation, circumcision and other legal rites, and of his baptism.

1. Christ Comes into the World

With respect to the conception of Christ, he considers first the Mother conceiving; second, the child conceived and its perfection. As for the Mother, he considers her disposition to such dignity both on the part of her soul and on the part of her body. The fullness of sanctity disposes her soul which conquered (*vicit*) sin in every respect from her conception, and lust or the inclination of appetite was retrained (*ligatus*), and was completely extinguished and removed when she conceived Christ. Lust is said to be bound when by the extrinsic protection of God alone it is held back lest it should erupt in some inordinate movement, and to be extinguished when by the intrinsic subjection sense appetite remains subject to reason, as in the state of innocence. The latter was conferred on the flesh of the Virgin by the flesh of Christ when he was conceived. In her this gift first shown forth. The former she had from the beginning. (q. 27).

On the side of the body she was disposed in three ways. First, absolutely in herself and with respect to God by her most immaculate virginity, fixed by a vow, and intact (*illaesa*) while giving birth and after. He treats this in **q. 28**. Second, with respect to men by her espousal, accepting Joseph her husband: this in **q. 29**. Third, with respect to the angels in the annunciation, which was made to her by an angel, that she might consent to the maternity of God: he discusses this in **q. 30**.

After considering the Mother, he turns to the child conceived and his conception. Four things are taken up here. First, the matter or material principle from which this flesh was assumed and formed, both remote, as it was in progenitors according to the origin of matter, although not according to seminal reason, and proximate which was from the most pure blood of the Virgin, not from seed: of this he treats in **q. 31**. Second, he considers the active principle of this conception which was the power of the Holy Spirit operating immediately, overshadowing the Virgin and substituting for the power of seed, not generating in his own likeness, and therefore he was not the father of Christ: this in **q. 32**. Third, he considers the manner of the conception, namely that the organization came about in an instant by the infinite power of the Spirit (**q. 33**). Fourth, he considers the perfection of the child conceived, because in that instant the soul was united to the Word and had the fullness of grace and glory, as well as merit, or the act of free will (**q. 34**).

After the conception of Christ, his nativity follows, and he considers two aspects of it. First, in itself and according to the circumstance of place and time, and how it was fitting to the person by reason of nature (**q. 35**). Second, he considers its manifestation, both to the shepherds and the Magi, and in what order and for what reason this was done (**q. 36**).

The circumcision followed the birth, along with other legal matters that were observed with respect to the child, such as the Purification of the Mother and the offering in the temple (**q. 37**).

Finally, he treats the baptism of Christ, which completes his entry into the world; from that point begins the process of his manifesting himself to the world. It was necessary for the baptism by John to precede both in order that Christ might be baptized and that men should become accustomed to baptism as Christ institutes it and thus be disposed to penance. So he first treats the baptism by John as something preparatory (**q. 38**). Of Christ's baptism, its circumstances and the testimonials whereby he is declared to be the Son of God, he treats in **q. 39**.

2. Christ's Life in the World

In the second place, Saint Thomas treats of Christ's conduct in this life. First, he speaks in general of the manner of his living (*conversatio*), not choosing an austere and solitary life, but one lived with men, but most virtuous and regulated in himself in order that others might come to him (**q. 40**).

Then he considers in particular the actions by which he both informs and reforms us. Some of his acts conquered the tempting devil, others instructed men in the doctrine he taught, though not in writing. Yet others concerned miracles he performed on behalf of other creatures, as a means by which the divine Word showed his divinity and confirmed us in the faith. Of the first kind, namely the temptation of Christ, he treats in **q. 41**. Of the second, his teaching, he treats in **q. 42**. The third, his miracles, he treats in three questions. First, the miracles of Christ in general and by what power and in what time he performed them, and how through them his divinity was sufficiently shown: **q. 43**. Second, specially of each of the four kinds of miracle, namely, those dealing with higher substance by expelling demons by his command; with respect to celestial bodies at the time of his passion; with respect to men, curing, enlightening, resurrecting; with respect to irrational creatures as by multiplying bread, converting water to wine, and the like: **q. 44**. Third, he treats in particular the miracle whereby he transfigured himself, showing his glory (**q. 45**).

3. Christ's Departure from the World

In the third place, Saint Thomas considers Christ's departure from this world by his passion and death. Here Saint Thomas takes up three things. First, the passion itself, both as to its fittingness for our salvation and showing forth God; and the species of passion, namely, on the cross; then the cruel sorrow and ignominy, which exceeded in gravity every suffering of this life (**q. 46**). Second, the cause of the passion, on the part of God, ordaining it out of his most high benignity, inspiring Christ with the will to suffer, and not protecting him from his persecutors, and on the part of men persecuting him and betraying him with consummate cruelty, the leaders, the people, and the gentiles as well (**q. 47**). Third is the effect of the passion with respect to its way of working for us, both meriting, satisfying, and redeeming, physically or efficiently working our salvation as an instrument conjoined to the Word (**q. 48**). Fourth, what the passion brought about for us, redeeming us from sin and reconciling us with God, thus earning for himself the highest exaltation of his name (**q. 49**).

After the passion, Saint Thomas considers his end and consummation, that is, his death, in which there was a true separation of soul from body, although not of both from the Word, by reason of which his body remained numerically the same and alive, by identity with the supposit (**q. 50**).

In the third place, he considers two things that followed on his death. First, with respect to his body, its burial (**q. 51**). With respect to his soul, his descent into hell and what he effected there, and the place to which he descended (**q. 52**).

4. The Exaltation of Christ

After Christ's departure from this world, there remains to treat his return to the world above and the glory with which he was crowned. Christ was exalted in three ways. First, through the glory of the resurrection and immortality; second, his ascension and the fittingness of the place; third, his sitting at the right hand of God in supreme dignity.

On the first exaltation, the resurrection, Saint Thomas considers four things. First, the resurrection with respect to its fittingness, time, and the cause that brought it about (**q. 53**). Second, he considers the quality of the resurrected body, namely, it is a true, complete, glorious body bearing wounds (**q. 54**). Third, the manifestation of the resurrection which was made clear by sufficient arguments, not to all, but to witnesses preordained by God (**q. 55**). Fourth, he considers the efficacious causality of the resurrection of Christ, both in souls, ". . . and rose again for our justification," Rom. 4, 25, and on bodies, "who will refashion the body of our lowliness, conforming it to the body of his glory," Phil. 3, 21 (**q. 56**).

The second exaltation of Christ was his ascension, whereby bodily according to his human nature (in which alone he was able to rise) he was exalted above the heavens and above every creature; and its effect on us, opening for us the way to heaven and dispensing his gifts to men (**q. 57**).

The third exaltation was in supreme dignity and power. In dignity, because he sits at the right hand of the Father, as a divine person in complete equality and with respect to his human nature he sits on the right, that is, established in the highest goods of God: of this he treats in **q. 58**. He is established in supreme power as the judge of the living and the dead. "All judgment he has given to the Son." John 5, 22. By his eternal generation he gives him power which is highest essentially; through the Incarnation he gave him in his human nature the highest power by way of participation, which is such that it extends to all men and angels who minister to him as a man and can receive from him at least accidental rewards (q. 59).

2. The Sacraments of the Church

Having explained the Incarnation of the Divine Word, he begins to treat of the means he left us to share in the efficacy of his blood. These are the sacraments, which he first considers in general, and then each of them in particular. The general consideration comprises five topics. First, the definition (quiddity) of sacrament; second, their necessity, which varies with states and thus cannot be treated until the quiddity of sacrament is known, which is one in genus; third, he considers the effect of the sacraments; fourth, their cause; fifth, their number.

a. In General

1. The Nature of Sacraments

With respect to the first, he treats the quiddity of sacrament by showing its genus, which is the genus of sign, as accepted and defined by those who in the Church passed on the notion of Sacrament: That it is a sacred sign, etc. So its genus is sign, and its difference is that it is a sacred sign, which is understood not of a sacred thing, as sacred in itself, but as making us holy. Thus the words practically and actively should not be taken actively in general and in the line of cause, for thus the difference would remove it from its genus, sign, but within the line of sign it should be understood of a practical sign as practically signifying, although it can take on the note of cause, but as adjectival and of another line, not as constituting the nature of sacrament. Since it is a sign with respect to men, who are led by sensible signs, it must be sensible, both on the part of the matter used and on the part of the form by which the signification is determined, namely, through words (q. 60).

2. The Necessity of the Sacraments

With respect to the second, he shows the necessity of these sacraments which arose after sin for which they are the medicine, and significative of redemptive grace through Christ. Hence just as in every condition after sin redemptive grace is necessary, so the sacraments, which are symbols testifying (*protestativa*) to this grace, and applicative, although more imperfectly before the Gospel than after and less efficacious. Before sin, man, though he gained knowledge through sensible things, did not receive grace: but he had received it from God in his very generation, nor was it given to him medicinally, and thus not sacramentally (**q. 61**).

3. The Effects of the Sacraments

With respect to the third, he considers a twofold effect. One is common to all the sacraments, namely, to give grace; another is special to some, namely, to imprint a character. He treats of the first in this question, both the thing caused, which is grace, not as commonly meant but as sacramental, that is, as in a special way medicinal of sin and healing by the aid of God and by participation in the redemption of Christ in the Christian life. He also treats the mode of causality of this grace, which from the genus of sacrament is only a practical sign, for which it suffices to signify grace as conferred by its manifestation and presence although not by itself: such were the sacraments of the Old Law. Evangelical sacraments, because of the effectiveness of the work done, signify grace not only as giving and as showing but as themselves perfect symbols and instruments of the passion of Christ; the passion of Christ was medicinal, as an instrument physically joined to the Word, but also as separate instruments, since they also share in the efficacy of Christ's passion, although *sui generis* as sacraments they do not signify it as giving it of themselves. All this in **q. 62**.

Another effect is a character, which is not given by all the sacraments, but only by those which especially make men ministers of Christ and sharers in his priesthood for the valid giving and receiving certain sacraments and doing the things which belong to divine worship in the power of Christ.

Although morally one might badly receive or administer, he does so validly in virtue of the character. Thus there is impressed a spiritual sign by which he is conformed to the priesthood of Christ, as his minister, and therefore this sign does not pertain to the essence of the soul, as it is not ordered to elevating it in being, as grace does, but deputizing him to minister, and it pertains to the power of ministering that which belongs to Christian worship that they might truly and validly come about. This it is in intellect, not as a habit which rectifies a power and constitutes an agent cause in the manner of an efficient cause, but in a ministerial manner, participating in power, but not so that one well or badly but validly does and receives what belong to the Christian worship. Such a character is imprinted by three sacraments: baptism, confirmation, and orders, because these three deputize special ministers: baptism, for validly receiving the other sacraments and what pertain to the faithful; confirmation, for validly confessing and defending; orders, for validly ordering and giving the sacraments (**q. 63**).

4. The Cause of the Sacraments

With respect to the fourth, Saint Thomas considers the cause of the sacraments, not only the principal instituting and operating cause, which is God, and in a most excellent manner the humanity of Christ as his instrument, but also the ones proximately ministering, the men who are ministers of Christ (**q. 64**).

5. The Number of Sacraments

With respect to the fifth, he adds up the number of sacraments: there are seven, and compares them among themselves as to excellence and necessity, and ministry (**q. 65**). Here he beautifully connects the seven to natural life in which are founded: generation, strengthening, nutrition, healing from ills, convalescence, multiplication, governance of the community. To generation, baptism corresponds; to strengthening, confirmation; to nutrition, the Eucharist; to healing, penance; to convalescence from the effects of sin, extreme unction; to multiplying, marriage; to governance, orders.

b. In Particular

1. Baptism

This sacrament is discussed under two general headings. First, the sacrament in itself; second, what prepares for it.

Concerning baptism itself, four things are discussed: first, its nature; second, its minister; third, its subject; fourth, its effect. The nature of baptism is taken from its matter and form, namely washing with simple and natural water with the required form, which is: "I baptize thee in the name of the Father, the Son, and the Holy Spirit." This is explained in **q. 66**. The minister of baptism, by office and solemnity, is the priest or bishop, but in case of necessity other lesser ones, indeed anyone, who states the form and washes according to the correct intention of the Church (**q. 67**). Its subject is any man born into the world, for all of whom baptism is necessary; one must be born in order to be reborn, either totally or with respect to some principal part outside the womb. The disposition of the subject, in the case of adults, is the desire to be baptized, and at least some contrition though not confession; in infants, the desire of their parents or guardians, and it is not licit to go against their wishes (**q. 68**). The effect of baptism is the remission of all sin and of the punishment due it, as well as the infusion of grace and virtue. Even if someone comes forward merely feigning desire, having removed the impediment by penance, it will have the effect of regeneration in virtue of the baptism received (**q. 69**).

As for preparation for baptism, he considers two things. First, that which in the Old Law prepared for baptism by way of figure, namely, circumcision, its rite and effect, namely, how it took away sin, even in little ones in the faith of Christ expressed in that sign, by its presence though not by its efficacy (**q. 70**). Second the preparatory ceremonies to our reception of baptism, such as exorcism and catechesis (**q. 71**).

2. Confirmation

One question comprises everything pertaining to this sacrament, first, its nature with respect to its matter, which is the oil of chrism made of oil and balsam blessed by the bishop, and with respect to its form, which is: "I sign you with the sign of the cross, etc." Second, its minister, who is ordinarily the bishop, but by commission of the Pope it can be a priest. Third, its effect, namely, the character and strengthening grace. Fourth, the receiving subject, namely, all the baptized, and on a determinate part of the body, namely, the forehead, lest those who confess the faith should blush (**q. 72**).

3. The Eucharist

Saint Thomas distributes the vast matter of this sacrament under seven headings treated through eleven questions, in this order: First, he considers this sacrament with respect to *whether it is* (*an est*), disputing its necessity, institution, and what prefigured it. Second, its matter, both remote, which is the bread and wine, and proximate, which are the consecrated species containing Christ; thus it was necessary to treat and explain this conversion. Third, its form. Fourth, its effects. Fifth, its recipients, and its use. Sixth, its minister. Seventh, the rite and mode of the sacrifice.

a. Its Necessity

Having supposed that the Eucharist is the sacrament containing the body and blood of Christ under the appearance of bread and wine, signifying grace through eating, Saint Thomas discusses the unity of this sacrament, both specific, which is in the manner of a banquet, made up of several kinds of things ordered to dining, and enumerated, that is, in what kind of consumption it is found, whether in the sacrament as ordered to the unique consumption when it is actually taken, or from the physical and material multiplication of the hosts when it is not actually consumed. He also treats of the necessity of this sacrament, which is not necessary by the necessity of a means as to its actual consumption, as baptism is regenerative, and thus by reason of its effect and reception necessary. But the Eucharist is nourishing and a food and thus its consumption supposes and does not give life. Its final causality, however, is necessary by the necessity of means with respect to the other sacraments, that is, all the others are ordered to what consummates them, insofar as its proper effect is to unite us in Christ, apart from which union we have no life. "He who eats my flesh remains in me and I in him." (John 6, 57) "Though many we are one body who participate in the one bread and cup." (1 Cor 10, 17) Although this unity is given by the other sacraments, this is as ordered to the Eucharist, to which it is properly attributed. By reason of this ordering, the other sacraments are called a wish to receive the Eucharist, not an express wish but in that they are as such ordered to the Eucharist as to their end (q. 73).

b. The Matter of the Sacrament

Four questions arise as to the matter of the Eucharist. First, he explains its remote matter, which is unleavened bread and wine from the grape, mixed with a little water, although that is not necessary for the sacrament but is so by precept (q. 74). Then he explains the proximate matter, which is the consecrated species containing the body of Christ by transubstantiation of the bread and wine placed there, about which it is necessary first to explain the conversion of the bread and wine, and then what follows on it.

First, then, he explains the conversion showing that it is given because the body of Christ is truly here, and not by any local motion deserting the heavens and acquiring a place in many hosts, but remaining in heaven. Therefore it is necessary that he be here through this that the bread is converted into him, and not by a formal conversion, for then only the form of Christ, his soul, would be introduced into the matter of the bread, and thus not the body of Christ, which is in heaven, but some other body, having acquired his soul *de novo* by its introduction into the matter of the bread, would be here. There remains therefore that there is the conversion of the whole substance of the bread into the whole preexisting substance of the body of Christ, the formal term of which is the body as converted from bread, not as produced, and thus *de novo* depending on God by reason of a new conversion of bread, nor by reason of a new existence. Hence the bread is not annihilated, because it does not fall into absolute nothingness, but into the body of Christ, which is something though it is not bread, just as every term *to which (ad quem)* is nothing of the term *from which (a quo)*, but not absolutely nothing (**q. 75**).

Two things follow on this conversion. First, in the body of Christ, a mode of existing sacramentally; second, in the species of bread and wine, a mode of existing per se without a subject. With respect to the first, that sacramental mode in which Christ exists here involves four things. With respect to the totality of the substance in which the conversion comes about, because the whole substance of the body of Christ is here, although some things from the force of the meanings of words, namely, what the words directly express, and some things by way of concomitance, namely, what of the thing expressed by the words is linked in reality but are not signified. Second, with respect to the correspondence with the quantity of the host: because the body of Christ is not in this manner quantitative, although its quantity is here, but in the manner of substance, whole in whole, and the whole in every part, because the conversion of the bread, however small, does not come about in part, but into the whole body of Christ. Third, with respect to place and motion: because he is not here circumscriptively in place nor as something locally mobile as such, but is moved accidentally with the motion of the species. Fourth, he is not here in a visible and sensible manner, because not in an extended manner, without which he cannot be sensed. He treats all this in **q. 76**. As for what follows in the species of bread and wine, namely, that they are accidents without a subject, he treats in **q. 77**, where he considers how these accidents remain both in being and in acting. In being, they remain outside the subject: for they do not inhere in bread because it is destroyed, nor in the body of Christ, because it is not capable of having the accidents of bread; nor in the air through which they move, for the same reason. Therefore they remain preserved by God in the being they had before, without dependence on the subject they had. In acting and being acted upon, they are in the same manner as before, because in lieu of a subject the quantity is sustained as such, and thus it acts and is acted upon until the corruption of the species (**q. 77**).

c . Its Form

With respect to its form, he shows what is the fitting form of
each species; some things are due to its substantial quiddity,
some to its integrity; and how their signification is verified
and caused by the word "this," and what power is impressed
on them instrumentally by God for this action, is treated in
q. 78.

d. The Effect of the Eucharist

He considers the effect of this sacrament, which is grace feed-
ing and uniting us to Christ, completely in another life and
inchoatively in this. Hence the effect of this sacrament is the
attainment of glory through the mode of ultimate union, fervor and the perfection of charity which unites us to Christ,
and by way of consequence the taking away of venial sins
and preservation from sins. It does not directly take away
mortal sin, because it presupposes the fervor of charity, and
food presupposes life, it does not first give it (**q. 79**).

e. Those Who Receive the Eucharist

Saint Thomas discusses the recipients of this sacrament, treating first consumption, both sacramentally and in reality, both
spiritually and by way of promise, the requirements and the
things which dispose men for this consuming. The whole
man should be disposed. In intellect, by having the judgment
of reason, not lacking discretion. In will, expelling all mortal
sin, not only by contrition, but also proving oneself through
confession. In body, there should be a fast, and no pollution
even in sleep for the sake of decency, unless necessity
requires. Finally, on the frequency and cessation from communion, **q. 80**. On its use with special reference to the way
Christ himself used it when he instituted this sacrament;
what fruit he had in himself; how he gives his body in an
impassible way, although in itself it is passible (**q. 81**).

f. The Eucharistic Minister

The minister is a legitimately ordained priest. He can validly
confect it even though he be bad and acts illicitly, though he
be degraded, excommunicated, heretical, etc., because the

power is never taken away but is an indelible character. And the sacrifice has the same power with respect to that which is founded in the person of Christ, the work being done (*opere operato*), not what is founded in the person of the priest (**q. 82**).

g. The Rite

The rite confecting this sacrament, and the notion of sacrifice, he treats by showing (i) the substance of this sacrifice. On the side of what is immolated it is the same as the sacrifice of the cross, but different in mode, because here blood flows in a bloodless and mystical manner, by consecrating separately the chalice and the bread. Therefore in the consecration of each species, insofar as mystically the blood is separated from the body, this sacrifice is perfected. (ii) He discusses the circumstances, ceremonies, and manner of sacrificing in **q. 83**.

4. Penance

The matter of this sacrament is broad, and Saint Thomas treats it by dividing it into six chief headings. First, he treats penance itself; second, its effects; third, its parts, which are contrition, confession, and satisfaction taken very broadly, where satisfaction is accomplished even by indulgences. Fourth, those receiving this sacrament. Fifth, its ministers and the power of the keys, as well as censures which pertain to binding and absolution. Sixth, on public and solemn penance.

a. The Nature of Penance

There are two things in penance, the note of sacrament and the note of virtue. He treats the sacrament in **q. 84**, where he shows its necessity, which is for all who have fallen after baptism, and similarly, matter and form. The acts of the penitent inwardly detesting sin is the matter and confessing externally what is detested. The form is absolution given by the priest. The sacrament of penance is defined thus: *the confession of sins with the absolution of the priest.* Of penance as it is an inner power, he treats in **q. 85**, showing how it is a virtue, indeed a special virtue. It is a virtue because one detests and sorrows over sin as it is against God and right reason. It is a special virtue because though it covers a most ample matter, that is, sin, it does so in a special way, that is, by way of recompense and expiation of the injury done to God. This is distinct from worship, for God should be worshiped even when he has not been offended. It is thus in the will (q. 85).

b. The Chief Effects of Penance
The chief effects of penance are four. The first is the remission of mortal sins. Second, is the remission of venial sins. Third, to impede the return of the sin forgiven. Fourth, the revivifying of merits and the recovery of virtues.

As for the first effect, Saint Thomas points out that sin should be taken away, and guilt, and eternal punishment as well as the depraved dispositions left by sin. Penance as a virtue removes guilt, dispositively; as a sacrament *ex opere operato*, instrumentally; in the same ways it takes away eternal punishment which accompanies guilt, changing it, however, into temporal punishment if penance is not fully satisfied. Depraved dispositions and habits are not immediately removed, but by the exercise of virtues in the contrary direction (q. 86).

In the second effect, he shows that the remission of venial sins does not require an infusion of grace, nor formally come about through it, because venial sins are not opposed to the habit of grace or its intension. They are removed therefore by some movement toward God, who virtually or formally is displeased by them, and thus the slow is not so slowed down by venial sin that it might be borne to God. Hence certain sacramentals instituted by the Church are said to take away venial sins, such as sprinkling with holy water, and the like (q. 87).

In the third effect, he considers that sins once dismissed, even if a man sins again, do not as such return. The stains taken away are not willed again, but others. Without will the stain of voluntary sin does not come about, and God neither imputes nor punishes sin unless there is a stain. One who sins seriously and after remission falls again, is said to fall into past sins only in a sense, from the circumstance of ingratitude (q. 88).

In the fourth effect, Saint Thomas considers penance to restore both the grace lost and the merits of what one did before: these are not forgotten by God who once accepted them, but sin only impedes a man from receiving the reward for them. They are said to revive when sin has been taken away by penance, because God restores their reward. Because a person can sometimes rise up again lukewarmly, little of habitual grace is given him again, since God gives grace in the measure of the recipient's disposition. Thus someone rising again from sin might not by dint of this receive the whole intensity of grace because of his lukewarm disposition, until he fervently disposes himself, either in this life, or as is probable on his departure from this life, when the separated soul more efficaciously acts, though it cannot merit new grace. On the recovery of the virtues he speaks in **q. 89.**

c. The Parts of Penance

St. Thomas began to consider the parts of penance, especially those which come from the side of its matter, as integral parts required for the sacrament of penance. These are three: contrition (under which attrition is understood), confession expressing sins with sorrow, and satisfaction. Of these and other parts he treats in general in **q. 90.**

*   *   *

Saint Thomas was prepared to explain them and other things in particular, bringing this Third Part to a good end, but he was prevented by Him who is the Ultimate End. God revealed to him secrets enclosed in the temple of his glory. Thus he did not write about the final object of theology, beatifying glory, having received it from the hands of God in recompense.

Index